XTREME FASHION

COURTENAY SMITH + SEAN TOPHAM

PRESTEL

MUNICH · BERLIN · LONDON · NEW YORK

PRESTEL VERLAG
KÖNIGINSTRASSE 9, D-80539 MUNICH
TEL. +49 (89) 38 17 09-0, FAX +49 (89) 38 17 09-35
WWW.PRESTEL.DE

PRESTEL PUBLISHING LTD.
4, BLOOMSBURY PLACE, LONDON WC1A 2QA
TEL. +44 (020) 7323 5004, FAX +44 (020) 7636 8004

PRESTEL PUBLISHING
900 BROADWAY, SUITE 603
NEW YORK, NY 10003
TEL. +1 (212) 995-2720, FAX +1 (212) 995-2733
WWW.PRESTEL.COM

LIBRARY OF CONGRESS CONTROL NUMBER: 2004097293

THE DEUTSCHE BIBLIOTHEK HOLDS A RECORD OF THIS PUBLICATION IN THE DEUTSCHE NATIONALBIBLIOGRAPHIE;
DETAILED BIBLIOGRAPHICAL DATA CAN BE FOUND UNDER: HTTP://DNB.DDE.DE

PRESTEL BOOKS ARE AVAILABLE WORLDWIDE. PLEASE CONTACT YOUR NEAREST BOOKSELLER OR
ONE OF THE ABOVE ADDRESSES FOR INFORMATION CONCERNING YOUR LOCAL DISTRIBUTOR.

EDITORIAL DIRECTION: PHILIPPA HURD
PICTURE RESEARCH AND MANAGEMENT: SABINE SCHMID
DESIGN, LAYOUT, AND TYPESETTING: SMITH, LONDON
ORIGINATION: DEXTER GRAPHICS, LONDON
PRINTING: PASSAVIA DRUCKSERVICE, PASSAU
BINDING: UEBERREUTER

PRINTED IN GERMANY ON ACID-FREE PAPER.
ISBN 3-7913-3175-2

AND FASHION
FOR ALL

once upon a time there was a widespread belief that fashion started on the catwalk and trickled down to the нigh street. тhe rich and beautiful dictated the trends and the plebs did their best to keep up. тimes have changed.

Haute couture houses, upmarket boutiques, exclusive department stores, and glossy magazines are no longer the dominant forces to shape the way people dress. More and more, fashion is dictated by the people who actually wear it. This shift in influence from insider "big names" to little-known outsiders has given us an interest in creative people from beyond the confines of *haute couture*. This book brings together designers, artists, activists, inventors, manufacturers, and others who are putting fashion out into the world in an engaging and accessible manner—imaginative people who are using the language of fashion to express their own ideas about who they are, where they place value, and how they perceive the world in which they live.

High fashion by its very nature is extreme. Many superstar designers and their celebrity clients employ shock-and-awe tactics to pop flash bulbs and grab headlines. Although often exquisite, these staged outbursts mainly pander to the mass media's appetite for drama and attention. By contrast, extreme fashion for us is not about self-aggrandizement, theatrical gimmicks, fickle trends, or "wackiness." It's about clothing that lays down a challenge to accepted norms. The majority of projects gathered together in this book are neither weird-looking nor loud, some might even seem banal, but appearances can be deceiving. We're not really interested in this season's look, new blacks, or disappearing hemlines. For us, fashion is a visual language that people employ to communicate with each other. Furthermore, it's about creating an identity and a space in response to the culture we inhabit. Fashion, as we see it, is not simply a passive signifier of preordained taste but an active means of social correspondence.

There is a one-size-fits-all mentality in mainstream fashion that is touted as the epitome of universal good taste—at least for one season or until the dictators of beauty and hipness change their minds. This frenetic cycle of "out with the old, in with the new" is a primarily western invention that dates back to the industrial revolution, the leisured monied classes it produced, and the grand boulevards of Europe. With great bundles to spend and generous avenues and parks in which to parade their wealth, the bourgeois industrial giants (and in particular their women) became the first modern-day conspicuous consumers and slaves to the latest fad. The more restrictive a woman's clothing was to wear, the higher the assumed rank of her husband. It was during this time that the bone corset, which produced the famous s-shaped curve on women's bodies, became a fashion staple. It was a shape that severely limited movement and was only really suitable for lazy afternoons spent drinking tea and eating cake.

To dress outside one's class was to somehow pretend, or even worse, to lie about one's identity. It was *déclassé,* as an American etiquette book from 1878 stated: "we Americans are lavish, generous, and ostentatious. The wives of our wealthy men are glorious in garb as are princesses and queens…But when those who can ill afford to wear alpaca persist in arraying themselves in silk…the matter is a sad one."[1] This didn't stop outsiders, such as poet Oscar Wilde, from going against the grain (Wilde himself dressed like a spoiled child and found merit in the mundane work clothes of American miners) but it did mark them as socially "off."

By the middle of the 20th century Paris had established itself as the home of high fashion. Its couture houses and their wealthy patrons took it upon themselves to instruct the rest of the world's women in how they ought to dress. Resourceful ladies of lesser means could follow the fashions of the day by running up their own home-made renditions of garments featured in the immensely popular vogue range of patterns. Later, the 1960s ushered in an explosion of fun, mass-produced clothing and accessories that actually celebrated the fact they were made from cheap, disposable materials such as plastic and polyester as opposed to the luxurious fabrics associated with *haute couture*. The consumer boom made aristocrats of everyone. The *hoi polloi* were presented with choice and through choice they began expressing their own tastes in matters of dress and personal identity on a scale that was previously unheard of. Designers including Paco Rabanne and André Courrèges expressed a desire to cater to the mass market rather than a pampered few. Even so, the illusion that good taste is the sole domain of the wealthy, the well bred, and the well educated persists— a belief that is trotted out time and time again in museum exhibitions of designer clothing and exclusive fashion boutiques that have the white walls and hallowed hush of art galleries.

High fashion, like a pedigree pooch, has a pure, unadulterated lineage but fashion, as we see it, is a mongrel. Fashion for us is neither pure nor self-contained. Moreover, it is a fluid and hybrid form produced by its interplay with other fields of inquiry including, but not limited to, art, science, architecture, graphic and product design, pop music, politics, and mass

And Fashion For All

sleazo

MONSTERS OF ROCK
IPOD VS BOOMBOX

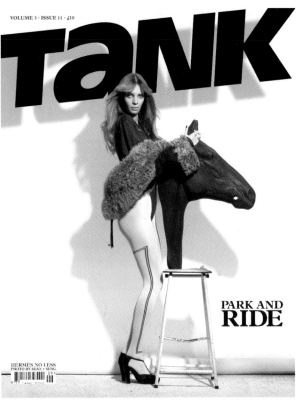

VOLUME 3 · ISSUE 11 · £10

TANK

PARK AND
RIDE

HERMÈS NO LESS
PHOTO BY SEAN + SENG

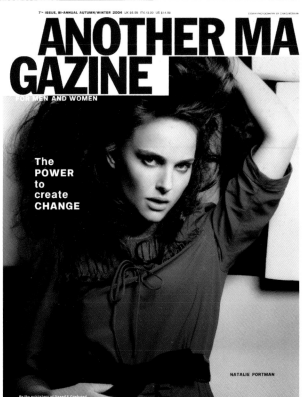

7ᵀᴴ ISSUE, BI-ANNUAL AUTUMN/WINTER 2004 UK £6.95 IT €.12.00 US $14.99

ANOTHER MA GAZINE

FOR MEN AND WOMEN

The
POWER
to
create
CHANGE

NATALIE PORTMAN

By the publishers of Dazed & Confused.

media. It is no longer valid to speak of "high-end" or "low-end" fashion. contemporary fashion, like contemporary culture, is all about the mix. The clothing, garments, and body coverings in this book deliberately cross disciplinary and cultural boundaries and often emerge from collaborations between individuals working in different contexts. Indeed, it is not possible to discuss fashion today without taking into careful account the cultural milieux in which it is produced. Global factors such as increased mobility and greater communication, and local factors such as climate and shared codes of behavior play decisive roles in how we dress ourselves. we've done our best to present a liberal and international cross-section of garments that respond to a variety of social situations and personal needs.

we have given over the first chapter titled "street Life" to projects that are characterized by their positive response to the inner city and fashions that celebrate the infectious DIY spirit of street culture. For centuries, wealthy men and women have used fashion as an agenda, whether to flagrantly flaunt their status or to demonstrate power, thus stylistic innovation traditionally filtered down from the highest echelons of society. Nowadays it starts at the bottom. street style has an attitude and a

credibility that simply cannot be recreated in a design studio. Rising against the onslaught of homogeneity brought about by globalization, are handmade garments, subversive accessories, outfits cobbled together from found materials, and other fashions inspired by the street that place emphasis on the local rather than the global community.

Related to this free-style approach is dressing up to become someone or something else. Fundamental to the second chapter, "Behind a Painted smile," are masks and other means of disguise used by activists, performers, and fetishists, among others, to subvert established orders or transform themselves and their identities. wearing a disguise gives license to behave in an extreme manner that might normally be deemed unacceptable or offensive. It can also be a very freeing experience that allows people to reveal facets of their personality they might usually keep hidden from view. This section looks at scenarios where clothes are used as screens or platforms on which individuals can adopt new personas and act and speak in ways they wouldn't dream of while dressed in their everyday clothes.

"To Protect and to serve," the third chapter in this book, explores garments that follow the

pathway forged by utility clothing. Here we delve into the realm of body coverings that perform functions, serve their users, and generally redefine the purpose of clothing. Robotic pants, transformable gowns, robust garments that offer protection from hazards as diverse as dog bites, gunshots, and inclement weather, and portable clothing "kits" whose modular pieces join together to form pants, skirts, tops, or handbags are among the multi-functional fashions investigated herein.

In the final chapter "Dress code," we look extensively at the language of clothes and the ways fashion is used to transmit signals. what we wear and how we wear it provides important information (or misinformation) to others about our sex, age, class, profession, and affiliations. Nowhere is this more apparent than at the door to a self-important nightclub, where subjective rules about who's in and who's out are governed by arbitrary dress codes enforced by burly security guards. As in Baudelaire's day, when the urban middle-class paraded their attire on the newly built boulevards of Paris, a stroll down any city street provides an opportunity to compare our own fashion sense with that of other people.

Throughout this book, there is an emphasis on socially conscious garments. while those

operating within the strict traditions of *haute couture* continue to drape pieces of fabric over a dummy, designers from other fields are creating garments with new materials and new methods of production. spanish artist Alicia Framis, for instance, has appropriated Twaron, an innovative dog-proof, bullet-proof, and fire-proof material, for a collection of clothes that is intended to give vulnerable women a new-found sense of security. Likewise, canadian designer stuart sproule has developed a line of mischievous clothing and accessories made with Dyneema-cored nylon, an ultra-strong material used in the manufacture of climbing rope and bullet-proof vests.

Environmental concerns, too, are expressed in projects where thriftiness and recycling come to the fore. when it comes to stylistic obsolescence and seasonal dumping, the fashion business is right up there with the auto industry as a well-known contributor to solid environmental waste. Leftover textiles, clothes that don't make it into broad public consumption, or garments that have simply fallen out of favor routinely meet in forgotten bales of "mixed rags" which must be reprocessed or dumped rather than passed on to the needy and homeless. An astounding 70%

And Fashion For All

of every ton of textile waste generated within the EU, for example, consists of discarded garments.[2]

Refusing to contribute to the fabric mountain, many designers are picking through it to find new inspiration in the shock of the old. Second-hand or unwanted clothes are the primary source material for a host of emerging designers whose motto is "never buy new." A related critical strategy is the rejection of contemporary fashion altogether by individuals who choose to dress themselves in the clothes of another decade or century. Dressing solely in the style of a time gone by requires continuity and commitment in identity construction and therefore is an effective means of short-circuiting the contradictory and constantly changing codes of commercial fashion.

Multi-functional attire is a further source of fascination. The marked rise in popularity of utility and military style clothing in the 1990s has helped spread the word that clothes can do more than look nice and cover our bodies. Not so long ago utility clothing and military surplus garb was more associated with cheapskates and radicals than young, upwardly mobile professionals. Today, even family-friendly GAP stores have their own line of combat pants. Soon after the first Gulf war, the seditious re-use of modern day battle dress was reduced to the must-have look of the season with Calvin Klein, Dolce & Gabbana, Donna Karan, and Jean Paul Gaultier all toting the style dubbed "military chic." The costume of the outcast became the costume of the conventional. Since that time, pocket-covered utility pants have proved especially useful to busy young urbanites who spend long hours away from home. Indeed, home might be only a small apartment where they sleep and store belongings. Clothing and accessories in such situations become extensions to the home and provide shelter from the outside world. These clothes are comfortable and styled for action—a far cry from the restraining clothes that endorsed inactivity at the turn of the 20th century.

Headway is also being made in the development of biomimetic fabrics that actually respond to climatic changes and the physical condition of the person wearing them. These materials mimic the behavioral patterns of our own biological systems, particularly the skin. In the desert, for example, a person wearing a garment made from a biomimetic fabric will feel equally comfortable in scorching daytime heat and freezing nighttime cold. Currently the technology is being developed for medical applications, space exploration, sportswear, and the military, but such innovations have a habit of turning up in the most unlikely places such as Corpo Nove's titanium-weave men's dress shirt, the "oricalco," whose fabric and shape react to shifts in temperature. When bunched together, the shirt forms and "remembers" wrinkles until being exposed to a current of hot air. Corpo Nove has also made significant strides in the everyday application of thermal insulation. Borrowing on technology from the aerospace industry, the Italian manufacturer has produced extremely warm but lightweight coats for civilians using Aerogel (which insulated the Mars Pathfinder in 1999) and liquid ceramic (normally applied to space-rocket engines).

Further examples of high-tech attire are expanding our expectations of what our clothes can do for us. Gadgets such as cellular phones, MP3 players, personal organizers, and computer games are shrinking at such a rate that they can be readily integrated into a handbag, jacket, or blouse. Outfits have been developed that are as wired as any modern-day home or office enabling unprecedented independence, security, and mobility. A number of designers are offering even greater autonomy by powering their gadget-packed garments with pocket-sized solar panels.

An obsessive interest in the urban experience permeates many of these multi-functional fashions. We are witnessing a move away from the paranoid "urban warrior" getups of the past decade, characterized by C.P. company's *Metropolis* Jacket (A/W 1997-98), toward almost comical forms of protest wear intended to offer protection and also provoke reactions. Temporary Services from Chicago have come up with giant inflatable heads and hands which allow them to protest in a friendly way while still offering visible statements should police restrain them behind barricades at great distances from protest sites. Temporary Services react to the city as if it were a playground rather than a battle-ground, but still manage to put their message across. Their ludicrous outfits provoke commentary and dialogue as well as enable people to claim their own spaces in a built environment used by many but governed for a select few.

A further reality of the urban environment is homelessness. We've included several projects by contemporary designers and artists who have taken it upon themselves to create outfits

for those who endure a fragile existence on the very fringes of society. The rejection of potentially lucrative clientele in favor of down-and-outs seems an increasingly popular gesture made by designers who want to align themselves with the deprived rather than the privileged. Instead of using fashion to try and permanently resolve the problem of homelessness, the creative people operating in this area are using clothes to draw our attention to a community that is usually ignored. Again, this recalls the manner in which the urban environment is often governed to create an attractive façade for the benefit of big businesses, rather than the diverse groups of people who make up the urban community.

Fashion impresarios, like businessmen, tend to think big, establishing global empires and forging networks to other institutional structures. In Germany, for example, fashion is regulated by the Ministry of Economics and Trade rather than the Ministry of Culture, diminishing design to a purely economic pursuit.³ We are interested in creative individuals who have forged their own paths and are working around, in parallel to, or outside of the fashion system altogether, often with very little money. There are many emerging talents from a variety of backgrounds who prefer to produce on a small independent scale, who understand that fashion plays a cultural and social role, and who believe that the best way to get a project off the ground is to launch it oneself. These individuals and modest teams are representative of a globally expanding "do-it-yourself" ethos whose adherents view the role of fashion within a broader, international context of public space, media, popular culture, and politics but who do not nessarily see the need to relocate to the hip fashion centers to try and "make it." On the contrary, many of these designers are staying put and demonstrating a strong commitment to the communities in which they are located, bolstering local work forces and, more importantly, bringing fashion back down to a human scale.

A great number of artists, designers, and social activists seek a broader role for fashion and their modest offices or flats are quickly becoming the new centers of fashion production. A shared understanding among all of these emerging creators is that fashion is not what walks down the runways in Milan, Paris, London, or New York but a reflection of what is happening "out there." Young designers wishing to reach a more diverse audience have staged fashion shows on subway platforms, in clubs, and at the Salvation Army. Others forego the show altogether and just put their work out there on the street. The options for getting one's ideas into public circulation on multiple levels are limitless. It's simply a matter of making fashion maneuverable in the broadest sense of the term.

Our past experience at the receiving end of schoolyard taunts about our clothes has given us an acute awareness of the significant role that fashion plays in everyday life. Fashion can be viewed as a language with its own vocabulary and grammar. Individual garments may be seen as nouns, verbs, adjectives, and so on, until they are combined into an outfit to form a complete sentence. Outfits born of specific urban quarters and "dialects" allow people to communicate equally specific messages within that environment or community, messages which are often appropriated and used to mean something entirely different in another context. The spectacular rise of MTV has resulted in a variety of cross-cultural imitation such as rich skater boys from Chiswick, West London, trying their damnedest to dress like gang-bangers from the city of Compton, in South Central Los Angeles. The clothes and the manner in which they are worn might be identical, but the meaning is totally different.

As a language, fashion also has its own expletives. In 1975, fashion designer Vivienne Westwood and punk entrepreneur Malcolm McLaren, her partner at the time, were prosecuted under Britain's obscenity laws for "exposing to public view an indecent exhibition." The offending article was a T-shirt depicting a cartoon drawing of two naked cowboys. It appeared in the window of McLaren's shop, Sex, on London's Kings Road. The provocative sexual imagery that decorated the shop and the clothes it sold caused outrage among the British press, politicians, and public alike. It's hard to imagine any mode of dress or single item of clothing causing such a furore in today's climate of anything goes, but any man stepping out in the wrong part of town dressed in an effeminate shirt and make-up is at risk from verbal and even physical abuse. Zoot suits, biker's jackets, thong bikinis, Doc Martens, and even jeans have all at some point in the latter half of the 20th century caused outrage among high-minded moral guardians. The most alarming youth-culture looks tend to either carry with them an implied threat of violence or they blur the boundaries between the sexes. The hooded sweatshirt has to be the early 21st-century equivalent of the

"'Ello Joe. Been anywhere lately
Nah, its all played aht Bill.
Gettin to straight."

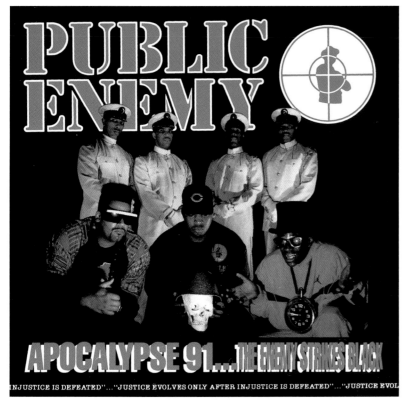

PUBLIC ENEMY

APOCALYPSE 91...THE ENEMY STRIKES BLACK

INJUSTICE IS DEFEATED"..."JUSTICE EVOLVES ONLY AFTER INJUSTICE IS DEFEATED"..."JUSTICE EVOL

CLOCKWISE FROM TOP LEFT

THE SHINY TRACKSUITS AND WRAPAROUND SHADES, POPULAR WITH BREAKDANCE CREWS AND BODYPOPPERS, DELIVERED A FUTURISTIC STYLE OF DRESS THAT LOOKED AS IF IT HAD DEVELOPED IN A VIDEO GAME.

ZOOT SUITS WERE AMONG THE EARLIEST REBELLIOUS MODES OF DRESS TO CAUSE OUTRAGE AMONG HIGH-MINDED MORAL GUARDIANS.

THE EMERGENCE OF HIP-HOP CULTURE IN THE LATE 1970S BROUGHT AN INTERNATIONAL FOCUS OF ATTENTION TO THE BRONX. MUSIC, MOVIES, AND IMAGES SUCH AS MARTHA COOPER'S DOCUMENTARY PHOTOGRAPHS HELPED ROCKET THE POPULARITY OF SPORTSWEAR AMONG YOUNG PEOPLE THE WORLD OVER.

FOLLOWING DOUBLE PAGES

LONDON-BASED DESIGNER VERONIKA KAPSALI IS DEVELOPING A COLLECTION OF BIOMIMETIC CLOTHING THAT AIMS TO HELP PEOPLE FEEL MORE COMFORTABLE IN THE URBAN ENVIRONMENT. THE CITY THROWS UP A MASSIVE RANGE OF CLIMATES AND CONDITIONS, FROM OVEN-LIKE UNDER-GROUND RAIL NETWORKS TO COOL AIR-CONDITIONED OFFICES. KAPSALI'S HIGH-TECH CLOTHES WILL BE ABLE TO COPE WITH SUCH EXTREMITIES WITHOUT HAVING TO REMOVE OR ADD LAYERS WHEN THE NEED ARISES.

biker's jacket. It is especially popular with unruly teenagers who want to keep their faces shrouded from the ever-watchful eye of CCTV, and has inspired designers such as Vexed Generation to raise concerns about the intrusive nature of video surveillance.

While Westwood and McLaren created expensive garments for their fashion boutique, bored teenagers up and down the UK were busy cultivating their own punk look. Punk, like the youth-culture movements that preceded it, was angry, energetic and offensive. Existing conventions governing good taste were ripped up and spat upon. Most important of all, however, was its DIY philosophy. The idea that the scene didn't need idols and that everyone involved could make a contribution was the fundamental message of the whole movement. Punks could make their own clothes out of old jeans, beer towels, bin liners, and safety pins—and that was cool. They didn't need stylish designer shirts to be accepted, like they did to get into the disco.

The same can be said of hip-hop culture. The early hip-hop scene grew out of the Bronx in New York. The Bronx of the 1970s was a district that looked as though a bomb had hit it. The culture that exploded from those ruins is now an international phenomenon, but it came from an area that was supposedly no good. In the introduction to the book *yes, yes, y'all*, author Nelson George describes how the Bronx at that time represented America's bitter rejection of the urban experience. "The South Bronx," he writes, "home to Yankee Stadium, wide boulevards, and miles of burnt-out buildings, became a national symbol visited by grandstanding politicians (like future president Ronald Reagan), ridiculed in Johnny Carson's nightly 'Tonight Show' monologues, and depicted in grim Hollywood flicks like Fort Apache—The Bronx."[4] While all this was going on, a bunch of kids who were essentially looking to have good times, developed a unique style of music, fashion, and art that later communicated their story to the whole world. The look they created consisted of what had, up until that time, been thought of as cheap, regular clothing, but hip-hop made it special. DMC, from rap act Run DMC, recalls: "we had on Lee jeans, shell-toe Adidas, Pro-Keds, Pumas, Kangol hats, sweatshirts, whatever was just common at the time, not the fly gear."[5] But it wasn't long before common sportswear became the fly gear. "People looked at us and could relate to us. The Cold Crush [Brothers] showed me that what my mother bought me was cool... we're normal guys, but we're good and this is who we be."[6]

Along with New York's basketball scene, the early 1980s' fitness boom, and European football, hip-hop helped rocket sportswear and sneaker brands to the international success they enjoy today. Sneakers such as the Nike Cortez, the Converse All Star Pro Model, and the Adidas Superstar (a.k.a. shell toes) achieved cult status while futuristic breakdance crews, decked out in shiny tracksuits and wraparound shades, looked as if they'd just stepped out of a video game. Customization was positively encouraged and kids would often modify or decorate off-the-peg clothes and shoes to make them their own. Just as they mixed, scratched, and rapped over existing pieces of music to create a wholly new sound, the pioneers of hip-hop created their own look by mixing up readily available garments in new and innovative ways. They didn't need a designer or a stylist to tell them what to wear, and neither do we.

What counts first and foremost is that fashion be created on one's own terms. This is the belief and *modus operandi* of virtually every "designer" in this book, all of whom work creatively around preexisting conditions and turn limitations into advantages to provide real alternatives to mainstream fashion. Style is relative and fashion is an immediate art that is free and available to us all. It is far too important to be presided over by a coven of tastemakers who wear black for every occasion. Neither of us has a background in fashion design or fashion history but every morning—like most other people—we make a decision about what we are going to wear. Some of those decisions might be described as misguided or maybe downright stupid, so we can hardly try and worm our way into the fashion cognoscenti. However, it is precisely these so-called fashion *faux pas* and fashion risks that shape our sense of self and create an identity that is truly our own.

1 Alison Lurie, *The Language of Clothes* (New York and Toronto: Random House, 1981), p. 116.

2 "Recycled clothing goes on and on," just-style.com, January 2, 2003.

3 Bakri Bakhit and Clara Brandenburg, "Unconventional strategies: Interviews with cultural producers from the fashion context," in *Atelier Europa* (Munich: Kunstverein München, 2004), p. 6.

4 Jim Fricke, and Charlie Ahearn, and Experience Music Project, *Yes, Yes, Y'all: Oral History of Hip-Hop's First Decade* (Cambridge, MA: Da Capo Press, 2002).

5 Ibid.

6 Ibid.

And Fashion For All

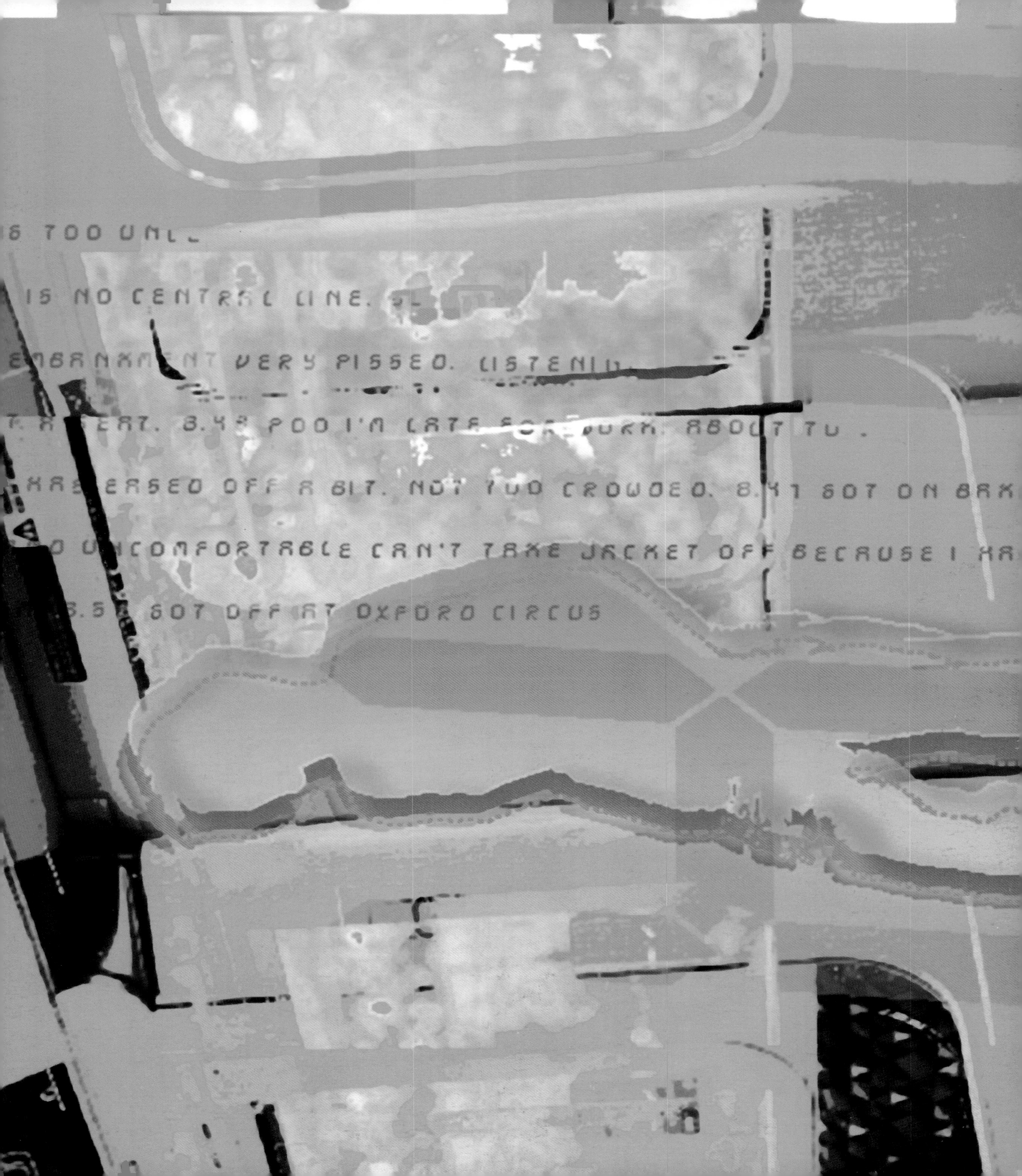

IS TOO UNC

IS NO CENTRAL LINE.

EMBANKMENT VERY PISSED. LISTENIN

T. SEAT. 8.42 POOJA LATE SOUTHWARK ABOUT TU.

KARSERSED OFF A BIT. NOT TOO CROWDED. 8.41 GOT ON BAK

O UNCOMFORTABLE CAN'T TAKE JACKET OF

GOT OFF AT OXFORD CIRCUS

BECAUSE I HA

CHAPTER 1

STREET LIFE

Despite all its illusions of grandeur the elite world of high fashion is quite content to take a peek over the fence to steal a few ideas from its hard-up neighbors. The big fashion houses moan constantly about people selling fake purses on the sidewalks, but they rarely think twice over pilfering ideas from those same city streets.

"street life" takes a look at projects that demonstrate a positive response to the inner city. The street is a hotbed of innovation that is rarely given the respect it deserves. Fashion designers were traditionally at the beck and call of the wealthy, but nowadays they're just as likely to be seen knocking up a survival suit for a wino. This remarkable shift in allegiance is telling of the powerful allure the street holds for those living in more salubrious parts of town.

catwalk shows are full of expensive copies of garments that earned their credibility on the streets. In many cases, the initial beauty of such garments (jeans are a prime example) was that they were practical and cheap, so it seems odd that the big fashion houses insist on producing their own very expensive and very impractical knock-offs. It's as though the garments can only be respected if they have the right price tag.

In this chapter cheap is definitely cheerful. Included here are several designers and artists, who have turned their backs on the high prices of high fashion to make clothing and accessories out of the most abundant and inexpensive materials. Demonstrating a resourceful attitude and embracing the DIY ethic of the street are artists and designers including JAM, Yuka Oyama, and Moreno Ferrari. Berlin-based Japanese artist, Oyama, for example, uses only materials that were once something else in her instant jewelry project, *schmuck quickies.* Italian designer Moreno Ferrari is best known for his work with lightweight high-tech fabrics but here he transforms bubble-wrap into bodysuits for the homeless. Taking the DIY spirit to the extreme is Manel Torres, a fashion designer and scientist who has invented a spray-on fabric that puts consumers in control of their clothing.

"street life" also includes outfits that raise important questions about how our streets are governed and for whom. Reclaiming the streets is a central theme in the clothing and accessories put forward by stuart sproule, Yomango, Temporary Services, and Vexed Generation. Canadian designer stuart sproule, for example, employs ultra-strong fabrics in urban outfits that transform the city into a playground, whereas chicago-based art group, Temporary Services, use giant homemade inflatable hands to give the finger to the authorities when they try to suppress rowdy political demonstrations. A playful mind-set characterizes these cheeky fashions that aim to subvert media stereotypes of "dangerous" protest groups and "treacherous" activists.

global news networks and reality cop shows are expert at generating hysteria over rising crime rates and terrorist attacks. paranoia has, for those who watch too much TV, become part of everyday life. when they're not waving the finger at foreigners, many of these panic-inducing broadcasts point to poverty-stricken inner city neighborhoods as the source of all society's nightmares. couple this with the recent rise in popularity among the mainstream of military-style clothing, tank-like sports utility vehicles, and those fortified compounds known as gated communities, and you have an alarming picture of a demilitarized zone emerging between the haves and the have-nots. this divide between "nice" neighborhoods and "bad" neighborhoods has resulted in whole communities been written off as no good. smashing through that divide and dismantling all those prejudices is tommy the clown, a young black male from Los Angeles's lower east side who loves nothing more than dressing like a clown and dancing like a crazy man. tommy and his crew cast aside those negative impressions of the inner city and spread the word that nice people live here too.

THOMAS JOHNSON, USA

TOMMY the clown, 1992 & ongoing

ABOVE THE COLORFUL EMBLEM PAINTED ON THE JACKETS AND T-SHIRTS OF TOMMY THE CLOWN'S CREW.

RIGHT, TOP ROCKO, A MEMBER OF TOMMY'S HIP HOP CLOWNS, PAINTED UP AND READY TO BATTLE.

RIGHT, BOTTOM TOMMY THE CLOWN WITH ROCKO OF THE HIP HOP CLOWNS.

FOLLOWING PAGES TOMMY AND THE HIP HOP CLOWNS TAKE THE STAGE AT THE BREAKIN' CONVENTION FESTIVAL, SADLER'S WELLS THEATRE, LONDON, MAY 2004.

THomas Johnson, a.k.a. TOmmy the clown, has created a phenomenon out of nothing. His outrageous style is a fresh response to the platinum-plated excess of mainstream hip-hop. It all started back in 1992 when JOHnson was asked by a friend to entertain the kids at her daughter's fifth birthday party. He put together a routine that mixed up magic tricks and party games with hip-hop jams and a crazy dance style that came to be known as "krumpin'." word of JOHnson's act spread rapidly around his neighborhood in the LOwer EAst side of LOS Angeles and TOmmy the clown was born.

TOmmy's reputation grew and he established a massive local following of kids of all ages who wanted to dress up and dance just like him. Demand was so great that he opened TOmmy the clown's HIP-HOP Academy of Dance as a space where he could work with the kids and help sharpen their face painting and krumpin' skills. TOmmy and his apprentices formed their own troupe called the HIP-HOP clowns and it wasn't long before similar crews began springing up across southern california. A vibrant dance scene has since developed from this community and, even though it constantly evolves as new ideas and attitudes are brought to it, the face paint and the costumes remain an essential part.

Krumpin' is a frenetic, high-octane dance style that mashes up influences as varied as break dancing, wrestling, kung fu, and the circus. competition between dancers is fierce, but always respectful and never violent. During a contest the teams of dancers face each other off just as they would in a break-dance battle. After that it's all about busting moves and making the best impact. The costumes and the face paint jack up the visual intensity of the dance and give it the look of a Mexican wrestling match. TOmmy is known for dressing like a typical clown in ludicrous shirts and a giant rainbow-colored Afro wig, but other members of his crew have taken the style to another level. They wear XXL T-shirts and ultra-baggy jeans in a look that resembles a street-style revamp of the traditional, oversized clown costume. The most striking factor, however, is the facial decoration—it looks like war paint. In a battle situation the dancers are able to adopt new identities behind their painted faces. They can transform themselves into whoever or whatever it takes to beat their rival. At a time when mainstream hip-hop seems obsessed with flagrant displays of wealth, TOmmy the clown and all the krumpin' kids are testament to the fact that you don't need thousand-dollar diamonds to dazzle.

Thomas Johnson, USA

Flee, 2003

why take the stairs when you can leap out of the window? stuart sproule's *Flee* collection throws down a challenge to the ways we are made to travel around the built environment. The canadian artist and designer fears that office blocks, municipal buildings, and whole cities have grown too authoritarian and we are no longer able to move freely around them. The items that make up the *Flee* range of products encourage people to think more creatively about the way they navigate streets, corridors, and other transitory spaces.

Flee has a tough, utilitarian look that underlines its confrontational stance. It consists of four separate products: *Escape*, a handbag made from knotted climbing rope; *swing*, a shoulder bag that can be used as a swing; *challenge*, a jacket incorporating a climbing rope and harness; and *suspend*, a pair of pants that also becomes a swing. whether it's scaling the face of an office block or swinging under a bridge, any of the four elements can be used to hook up to an existing structure and exploit it in a new way. Flee is a reaction against the regimented order of the city and a means of fracturing the grid.

sproule developed the project while he was studying at the Design Academy in Eindhoven in the Netherlands. "Eindhoven is unreal," he insists. "There are signs and signals for everything. It's a very ordered place, but very liberal and free at the same time. it's an unusual combination." The *Flee* collection of products gain their strength and durability from advanced textiles such as Dyneema and Kevlar, materials more commonly associated with the military or rescue services. where other designers employ these tough fabrics in garments that offer security or protection, such as bulletproof vests, sproule uses them in products that encourage creativity and liberation.

"we just don't think about it. we don't think about how we are controlled," argues sproule in response to the way we are herded around buildings and cities. A sloping concrete bund will steer people in one direction, while an array of chevrons will drive them in another. They represent discreet ways of keeping people on the move. The *Flee* collection is about taking control of your environment rather than allowing it to control you. It can transform a routine trip to the office into an exciting adventure. the project celebrates risk and shares with graffiti artists and base jumpers a vision of the city as a vast playground.

LEFT AND OPPOSITE *ESCAPE*, A HANDBAG MADE FROM LOOSELY KNITTED CLIMBING ROPE.

BELOW SPROULE'S "HOW-TO" DIAGRAMS OFFER A FEW SUGGESTIONS AS TO HOW THE VARIOUS ITEMS IN HIS *FLEE* COLLECTION CAN BE USED TO INJECT A SPIRIT OF ADVENTURE INTO EVERYDAY TRIPS AROUND THE CITY.

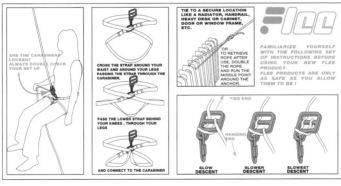

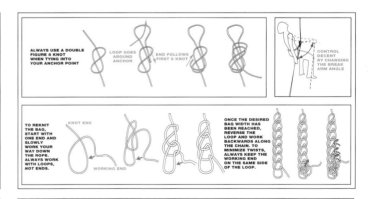

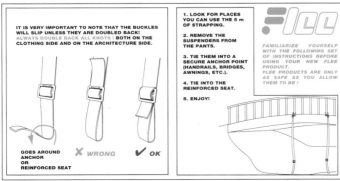

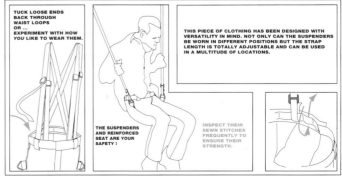

RIGHT AND OPPOSITE

SUSPEND, A PAIR OF PANTS THAT TRANSFORM INTO A SWING, AND *CHALLENGE*, A JACKET FITTED WITH A HARNESS AND CLIMBING ROPE THAT CAN BE USED TO SCALE BUILDINGS.

stuart sproule, canada

L'uomo-canoa (The Man-Canoe), 2002
In Trasparenza: vivere ed Abitare L'inconsistente (In Transparency: To Dress and to Live the Insubstantial), 2001

Moreno Ferrari has a strong reputation for designing transformable garments aimed at people on the move. For the *In Trasparenza* project the Italian designer has used sheets of plastic bubble wrap to make a series of rugged outfits for homeless people. The material is cheap and disposable yet also durable, insulating, and very lightweight. It is commonly used to protect fragile artifacts and highlights the vulnerable and fragile existence of the homeless community.

The garments are designed to be worn over other layers of clothing to offer protection from the cold and damp. Multiple pockets, also made with bubble-wrap, can be attached and removed using velcro to make it easier to carry and store personal possessions. Extra layers of the material are used to reinforce areas including the elbows and shoulders of the bodysuits to make them more resistant to wear and also act as a shield against physical abuse.

The bubble-wrap suits aren't so much about solving the inordinately complex problem of homelessness as they are about creating personal space for those who have none. The outfits deliver, as Ferrari puts it, "a privacy that a home offers and a street denies." The clothes behave like buildings in that they form an intimate space where a person might eventually find the security of a home.

In Ferrari's world clothing becomes a refuge equipped with a few essential tools and the odd home comfort. *L'uomo-canoa* is a prime example. Ferrari has devised an adaptable outfit that can be worn as a suit of clothes, slept in like a bed, erected as a shelter, or inflated to form a small boat. The designer describes it as, "a contemporary technological ark," and a "moving architecture of the water and the land." *L'uomo-canoa* is an outfit that equips its user with tools to cope with a constantly shifting environment. It offers comfort in the form of shelter and a buoyant vessel for transportation.

Homelessness is a prominent theme in much of Ferrari's work, not in terms of destitute people living rough on the streets but in the way that city centers and other places are dominated by transient spaces where people are subtly urged to stay on the move. A homeless person is the extreme victim of this situation because everyone else has a home to go to. Those left behind just have to keep walking.

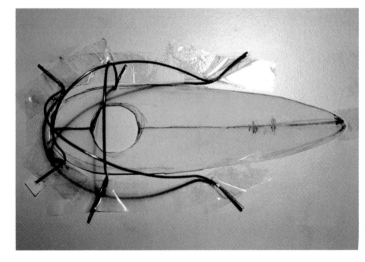

Moreno Ferrari, Italy

LEFT THE BUBBLE-WRAP SUIT RESEMBLES AN ASTRONAUT'S SPACE SUIT, AND LIKE A SPACE SUIT IT OFFERS PROTECTION TO THE BODY AND STORAGE FOR ESSENTIAL SUPPLIES SUCH AS FOOD AND WATER. VELCRO IS USED TO HOOK THE LARGE POCKETS TO THE MAIN BODY OF THE SUIT. THESE DETACHABLE POCKETS ENABLE THE PERSON WEARING THE ENSEMBLE TO KEEP THEIR PERSONAL BELONGINGS SAFE AND DRY WHILE ALSO LEAVING THEIR HANDS FREE TO PERFORM OTHER TASKS.

YOMANGO, SPAIN

The Magic Bag, 2004
Porta-CD Skirt, 2004
Frying Pan Apron, 2004
Be Yourself!, 2004

RIGHT, TOP YOMANGO'S *PORTA-CD SKIRT* RESEMBLES A MAID'S APRON BUT IS IN FACT UTILITY CLOTHING FOR STEALING CDS.

RIGHT, BOTTOM YOMANGO'S *FRYING PAN APRON* HELPS ITS USERS PREPARE MEALS WITHOUT RUINING THEIR OWN POTS AND PANS. WITH THE HELP OF A ZIPPERED POUCH, NEEDED COOKWARE CAN BE "UN-PURCHASED" FROM ANY MAJOR DEPARTMENT STORE WITHOUT DETECTION. YOMANGO ENCOURAGES USERS TO "SHAKE THAT POT AND SHOW THEM WHO REALLY HAS THE PAN BY THE HANDLE!"

Yomango is the brand name of an anarchistic practice used by an international network of people with franchises in Chile, Mexico, and Argentina and fans all over Italy and Germany. In Spanish slang, the name means "I steal" and is, in fact, the combination of two distinct Spanish words "yo" (meaning "I") and "Mango," the name of a popular Spanish clothing chain. As part of their cause, Yomango promote civil disobedience through tactics such as stealing. This starts with their group's logo, which was lifted from that of Mango, and extends to a range of garments designed to help individuals shoplift. For Yomango, stealing isn't a crime but a means of self-realization. According to the group's credo, "shopping is an act of obedience. Yomango is your disobedient style."

The group use fashion as one of a number of strategies to reclaim individual choice and control from global producers. To do so, they parody the sales language and advertising images of industry brands but insert a very different message. As their website states, "Like all other major brand names, it is not so much about selling concrete stuff but more about promoting a lifestyle. In this case, the Yomango lifestyle consists of shoplifting as a form of social disobedience and direct action against multinational corporations."

Yomango's garments and accessories, aren't so much products as they are social strategies. The *Magic Bag,* for example, is designed to make objects "disappear" and can be constructed by anyone according to their own desires and needs. Yomango provides patterns for those who wish to stitch their own. A shoplifting tool that helps individuals "un-purchase" needed products, the *Magic Bag,* like the *ultimate Jacket* on pages 62–63 of this book, has a multitude of secret pockets such as those found in the costumes of magicians or other sleight-of-hand tricksters. It is therefore perfect for tucking away treasured retail finds:

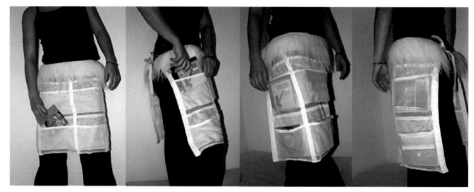

"The packet of coffee or that expensive book you've just un-bought will have disappeared… and instead you'll be able to say 'oh, thank you for searching my bag! Here's that vibrator I've been looking for all week!'"

A related idea for outsmarting retailers is Yomango's *Porta-CD Skirt,* "the ideal accessory for strolling through a shopping center on weekends when you have nothing better to do." Tied around the waist like an apron, the skirt is made of a semi-transparent fabric with big, easy-glide pockets for accuracy and efficiency in whisking away one's finds. Once filled, the see-through pockets become visible statements about one's tastes and leanings. Yomango recommend "choos[ing] your CDs carefully to give your skirt a fabulous print."

The de-purchasing of consumer goods is promoted by Yomango as a "style" that goes beyond one season and has more to do with social engineering than fashion design. Their *Be Yourself* collection consists of as many items of clothing as one can "un-buy" by removing the electric alarms attached to them. The hole left by tearing the locks off becomes a logo in its own right, a symbol of coherence to Yomango values. "The stores think this [the alarm] will be enough to stop you unstealing them. But that hole in your jacket or pants where you rip out the alarm will actually become a sign of your special Yomango style."

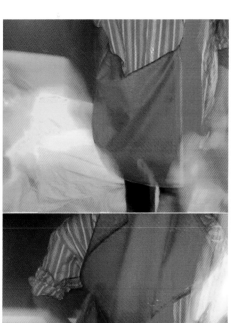

yomango, spain

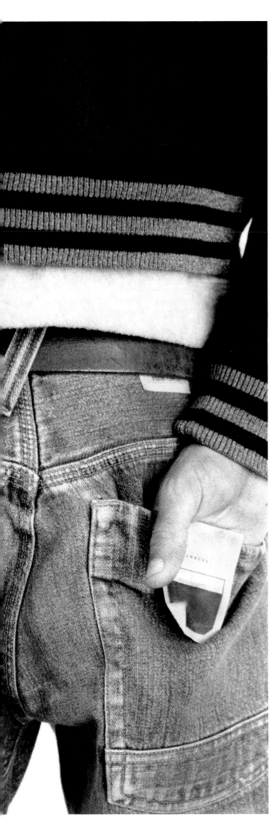

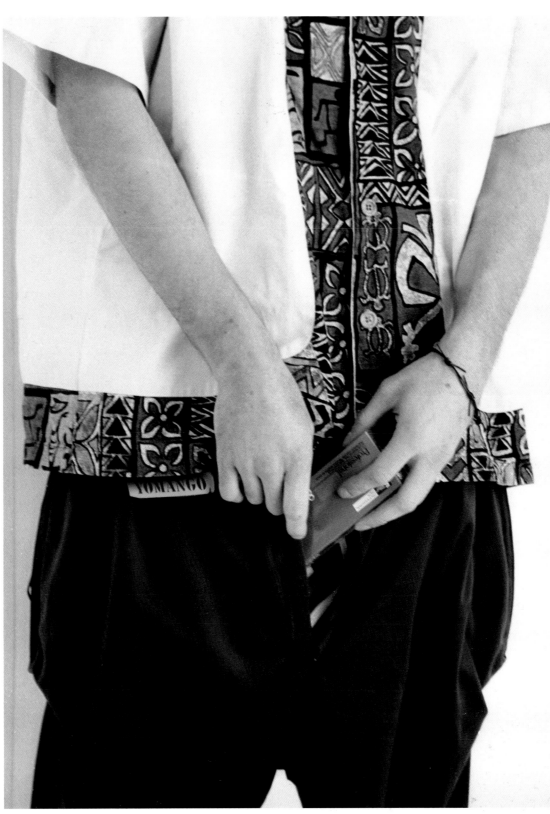

FAR LEFT *THE MAGIC BAG* IS A SHOPLIFTING DEVICE THAT RESEMBLES A REGULAR TOTE. IT CONTAINS THOUSANDS OF SECRET POCKETS THAT "WILL HELP YOU IF THAT ANGRY LOOKING MAN IN THE UNIFORM OR THAT STICKYBEAT GIRL AT THE COUNTER LOOK AT YOU SUSPICIOUSLY AND ASK TO LOOK INSIDE."

CENTER YOMANGO ENCOURAGE EVERYONE TO BE THEMSELVES BY CREATING THEIR OWN UNIQUE STYLE. ONE WAY OF ACHIEVING THIS IS BY RIPPING THE SECURITY TAGS OFF OF CLOTHING AND LEAVING THE HOLE OPEN AS A SIGN OF GOOD FASHION SENSE.

NEAR LEFT *.ZIP!* IS YET ANOTHER MEANS OF CONCEALING STOLEN GOODS. THE PANTS HAVE A FALSE ZIP THAT CONCEALS A BIG POCKET FOR LARGER ITEMS.

schmuck quickies, 2002 & ongoing

BELOW LEFT AND CENTER
ARTIST YUKA OYAMA IS
INTERESTED IN CLOTHING,
JEWELRY, AND ACCESSORIES
OF THE STREET "BECAUSE THEY
ELUCIDATE THE CHARACTER,
TASTE, AND STATE OF MIND OF
THEIR WEARERS...I PREFER
PEOPLE WHO WEAR WHAT THEY
WANT. PEOPLE WHO FEEL GOOD
IN THEIR CLOTHES. IN OTHER
WORDS, PEOPLE WHO ARE
INDEPENDENT OF TRENDS
AND THE MEDIA."

RIGHT JAPANESE "CLIENT"
SHINICHIROU TAKAHASHI WAS
QUITE PLEASED WITH THE
RECYCLED BODY ACCESSORIES
OYAMA MADE FOR HIM: "IT
LOOKS LIKE A BUG. GREAT!
ADD SOME MORE OF THAT
BLUE STUFF. I'VE GOTTA GO
TO A PARTY IN TOWN."

OPPOSITE, LEFT HARUYO
HIGUCHI: "I WANT TO LOOK LIKE
AN OIRAN...I LIKE THIS. I WILL
PLACE THIS IN FRONT OF MY
ALTAR ON NEW YEAR'S DAY."

OPPOSITE, RIGHT NAOKO
KANEZUKA: "I WOULD LIKE
TO HAVE A PIECE LIKE A PET
THAT YOU CAN CARRY AND
WALK AROUND WITH."

**FOLLOWING PAGES, FROM LEFT
TO RIGHT** A TRIO OF FRIENDS,
KAZUHIKO MATSUZA, AND A
WADA COUPLE.

Yuka Oyama creates spontaneous and highly personal jewelry and body accessories—free of charge and in a matter of minutes—for anyone who wishes to participate in her performances. *schmuck quickies*, as the Berlin-based artist calls the events, have taken place in art spaces in Munich and Berlin, Germany, Meran, Italy, and most recently in Niigata and Tokyo, Japan.

Oyama's "schmuck" (German for "jewelry") is cobbled together from odds and ends and almost anything that has been discarded or abandoned. She is constantly on the look-out for new finds, which she collects, sorts, and stores in self-designed bags and carts, not unlike those of her high-fashion colleagues. But this is where the comparison ends, for oyama is not the least bit interested in the latest trends. Her *modus operandi* is "never buy new" and everything she makes is composed of local materials or objects that have lost their original use. "One of the simplest forms of jewelry is to take things that are available in one's environment and to put them on the body," says oyama. "Making jewelry that is individual can also mean reassessing what is available in our everyday life."

Even so, oyama's unique pieces are not so much jewelry in the traditional sense as literal extensions into physical space of the wearers' desires and personalities. In the Japan performance, seen on these pages, she

created all manner of attachments, extensions, additions, and protrusions—using plastic visors, egg cartons, tennis rackets, even mini-blinds—which demanded as much space and attention as the person wearing them.

Oyama is highly sensitive to the wishes and idiosyncracies of her "clients" and is quick to point out that there used to be a time when a dialogue took place between dressmaker and dressed. Ideas, opinions, and even mundane topics were spoken about while bodylines were pinned down. This art of exchange has been lost in the mass-production of fashion, but oyama carries it on her one-on-one chats with clients. As she rummages through bags of raw materials, she asks questions, listens to what her sitters say, and tries to match their desires and physical attributes with appropriate materials. For shinichirou Takahashi, who wanted "to have the strongest look of all, so that no one can win me over," the result was tennis-racket appendages mounted to his body with tape.

In the end, clothes and accessories are what we want them to be. "In the march towards global standardization in our consumer society, producing things of the same quality and with no differences or gray areas have been encouraged, " says oyama. "Yet, we still hope to be different from others. Between these contradictions are *schmuck quickies*."

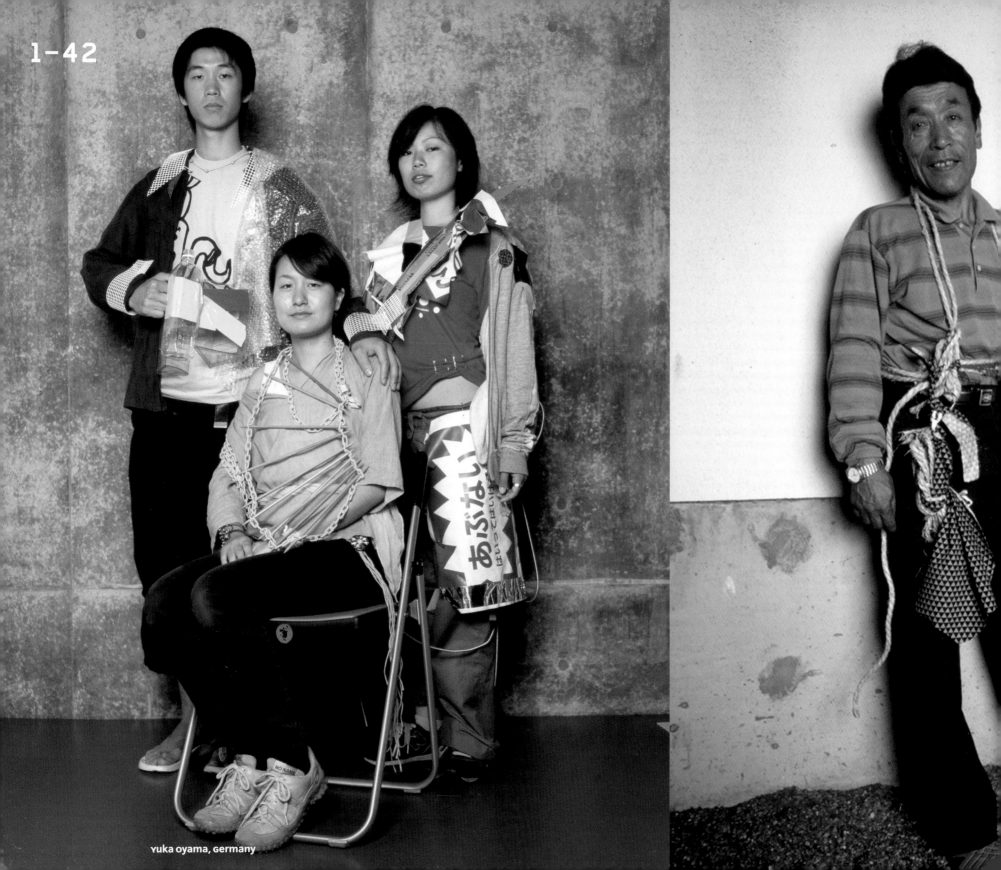

yuka oyama, germany

TEMPORARY SERVICES, USA WITH ZENA SAKOWSKI AND ROB KELLY

Midwest side story, 2002

BELOW AND OPPOSITE A LARGE INFLATABLE HEAD AND PAIR OF HANDS HELP MAKE ROOM IN A CROWD AND INSURE THAT PROTESTERS' MESSAGES WILL BE VISIBLE FROM BEHIND POLICE BARRICADES.

FOLLOWING PAGES SELF-CREATED MASKS MADE OUT OF PLASTIC BAGS ARE USED TO EXPLORE NEW IDENTITIES.

The *Big Head, Big Hands,* and *Masks* by chicago-based art group Temporary Services and artists Zena Sakowski and Rob Kelly are humorous examples of how attire can alter the way we perceive and use public space, in particular the street. Handmade from readily available materials—such as plastic grocery bags, tape, rope, electric and gas-powered leaf blowers, as well as miniature, battery-operated fans—the inflatable body parts and pull-on face coverings made their debut as part of the project *Midwest side story* that took place in chicago and various cities in Puerto Rico in 2002.

"we live in neighborhoods where street gangs are active, violent, and brutal," says Ts member Brett Bloom. "*Midwest side story* was loosely based on *west side story*, the musical by Leonard Bernstein and stephen sondheim, which offers some interesting dialogue about the uses of public space." In the musical, rival gangs on New York's upper west side vie for control of the public street. The Anglo Jets and Puerto Rican sharks carve out their turf through stylized dress, slick language, and

provocative dance movements. As the battle for space escalates, violence is thwarted by the sound of a policeman's whistle, an arbitrary authority that forces the gangs to flee.

In the case of *Midwest side story,* the role of arbiter was played by Temporary Services, sakowski, and Kelly, all of whom share the need to initiate change within their daily lives. Thus, *Midwest side story* offered a starting point for all involved to unleash their own form of positive mayhem in various public situations and contexts. As in the musical, Ts members along with sakowski and Kelly marked their positions by donning the comical inflated creations and handing out homemade masks. In response, passers-by could choose to wear a mask and join the act, or not. whatever the degree of participation, people were forced to stop and reassess their normal patterns of behavior and surroundings.

"The entire project was about creating disruptions in public spaces—getting people to act differently," says Bloom. "The inflatable devices did that in very similar ways to the masks....The masks worked really quickly to

change social situations whenever they were handed out. We also put them on statues and inanimate objects throughout our movements in the different city spaces of san Juan, Naranjito, and a couple of other places in Puerto Rico."

The *Big Hands* were also used during a 2002 protest against the Transatlantic Business Dialogue in chicago. Because demonstrators were sequestered behind police barricades at a great distance from the protest site, *Big Hands* proved quite effective in getting messages across from afar, especially when the individual fingers were arranged in the sign of "the bird." The hands were given to other protestors to wear to express their frustration and outrage with the TABD and the repressive police presence.

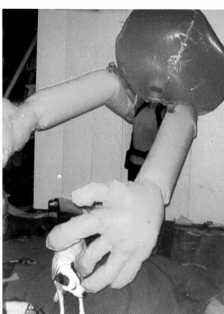

RIGHT AND OPPOSITE

AVAILABLE AS BAGS, BELTS, OR JACKETS, *NOON SOLAR* GARMENTS AND ACCESSORIES ARE EQUIPPED WITH MICRO SOLAR PANELS THAT ENABLE WEARERS TO POWER THEIR CELL PHONES AND GAMEBOYS WITHOUT RECHARGING AT A WALL SOCKET. CONCEIVED BY ARTISTS/DESIGNERS JANE PALMER AND MARIANNE FAIRBANKS, *NOON SOLAR* GARMENTS "ALLOW YOU FREEDOM OF SINGULARITY WHILE ALSO PROVIDING YOU WITH THE CAPABILITIES OF CONNECTING TO THE LARGER INFORMATION NETWORKING SYSTEMS OF OUR CULTURE."

Gameboys, cell phones, walkmans, and Palm Pilots are just a few of the devices that make our lives more mobile—or so it seems until they run out of juice and we have to find an electrical socket to recharge their batteries.

For artists/designers Jane Palmer and Marianne Fairbanks, who have been working together since 2000, this is a problem that can be solved easily by the sun. All of their *noon solar* bags, belts, and jackets are fitted with micro solar panels and 12-volt battery packs that store energy as their wearers stroll down the street. The technology is impressively simple and efficient. Solar panels, housed in weatherproof sheaths, are sewn onto the outside of clothing and bags and then connected to a small battery inside. The battery, in turn, is connected to a universal cigarette-lighter socket. Anyone with a cigarette-lighter adaptor and interchangeable tips for portable devices can use the garments and totes.

Although funky, flexible, and fun, JAM's garments are very much educated fashion responses to pressing environmental, political, and social concerns. Experts already predict that by mid-century fossil fuels will be depleted and replaced by other, more eco-friendly sources. JAM's garments and accessories anticipate this coming reality and are pragmatic, first steps toward living off the grid. According to Fairbanks and Palmer, the path to personal empowerment is all about kicking the oil habit. "We wanted to bring literal power to the individual," says Palmer. "A lot of it for us is being off the grid and having alternative energy sources."

An overwhelming sense of powerlessness, in fact, played a central role in the development of *noon solar.* Early on, it occurred to Fairbanks and Palmer that both were deeply dissatisfied with the political situation in the United States, in particular with an American president bent on war in the Gulf. At the same time, like so many other citizens, they didn't see any possibility for change or dialogue on the subject. "Decisions were being made, and it didn't really matter what an individual was saying," so the two roommates started talking to themselves about how "tangible and physical" power could be returned to everyday people.

The result is a product that they hope one day will be refined enough to produce on a mass scale and that will then trickle down into daily life. Until then, they are committed to refining the technology so that other designers will be able to integrate the product into their own garments and bags for wider distribution. After all, fashion need not be limited to theoretically enticing but dysfunctional get-ups. Rather, JAM demonstrate how, with determination, a DIY spirit, and a real-life cause, fashion can be applied to the greater common good.

VEXED GENERATION, UK

vexed parka, A/W 95
ninja hood and ninja high-neck tops
SAB coat, A/W 01

London-based fashion label Vexed Generation was at the forefront of the 1990s' trend for tough, urban street wear. The *vexed Parka* was part of the label's debut collection in 1995 and was designed in response to the heavy-handed tactics used by the authorities in the UK to control demonstrators at rallies against the criminal Justice Act in the early 1990s.

The parka closely resembles the body armor worn by frontline police officers and is designed to offer protection from physical assaults. Joe Hunter and Adam Thorpe, the designers behind Vexed Generation, noticed that when such demonstrations turn nasty, riot police tend to try and debilitate demonstrators by using their truncheons to hit them in the groin or around the lower back. The vexed Parka is padded to offer protection around the spine and kidneys and also comes with a between-the-legs fastening to shield the sensitive groin area. To ensure that the coat is as tough as it looks, the designers employ a slash-proof and fire-resistant nylon that was originally developed for use in blast-proof curtains and protective flak jackets. The designers used riot gear as their inspiration and from it developed a range of protective clothing well suited to cycling, riding scooters, and similar exposed forms of urban transportation. Concerns about the increasing use of CCTV play a major role in the shaping of Vexed Generation's *Ninja Hood* and *Ninja High-neck Tops*. Inspired by the bad-boy cool of hooded sweatshirts and zip-up tracksuit tops sported by teenagers the world over, the garments were designed to raise awareness about the use of video surveillance in public areas. The vexed garments have high necklines that can be worn over the lower half of the face to conceal the identity of the person wearing them. These clothes aren't designed to encourage criminal activity, but they help level out the playing field when those in charge start abusing their powers. More than anything they appear to express apprehension about the erosion of civil liberties such as the right to protest. Fashion is a means for the people behind Vexed Generation to communicate their ideas about pressing social and political issues to a wider audience.

LEFT THE *NINJA HOOD* AND *NINJA HIGH-NECK TOPS* HELP CONCEAL THE IDENTITY OF THE PEOPLE WHO WEAR THEM AND EXPRESS CONCERNS OVER THE PREVALENT USE OF VIDEO SURVEILLANCE. THIS SELECTION OF JACKETS ALSO ILLUSTRATES HOW THE DESIGNERS ARE KEEN TO MAKE FASHION CLOTHES WITH CYCLISTS AND SCOOTER RIDERS IN MIND.

OPPOSITE THE REFLECTIVE STRIPS ON THE *SAB COAT* INCREASE THE VISIBILITY OF THE WEARER AT NIGHT WHILE THE MULTIPLE POCKETS PROVIDE SECURE STORAGE SPACE FOR PEOPLE WHO NEED TO KEEP THEIR HANDS FREE.

vexed generation, uk

spray-on phenomena such as deodorant, shaving foam, and hair spray perform a fundamental role in our early morning routines. we've grown accustomed to discharging a fine spray from a pressurized container and applying it to our body, face, or hair. Manel Torres and his team at Imperial college, London, have taken this practice a step further with the creation of Fabrican, a revolutionary fabric that comes in a can. The idea is simple: you spray yourself with the pressurized liquid and it instantly transforms into a fabric as it hits your skin. Each squirt from the can sends thousands of tiny cotton fibers splattering against the contours of the body. These fibers bind together to form a disposable garment that, once finished with, cleanly peels away.

Perhaps the most radical attribute of Fabrican is that it removes the designer from the manufacturing process of clothing. "our appetite for speed of delivery shows no signs of slowing down," remarks Torres on the success of fast-food outlets, ready made meals, and instant noodles. Fashion, too, is a speedy enterprise but the manufacture of a couture garment can be very time-consuming and labor-intensive. "I want to speed up this production process," says Torres, "and offer consumers a tool with which they can effectively create their own clothing."

Designers such as Paco Rabanne experimented with disposable clothing back in the 1960s. His *Paper* dresses (1967) enjoyed considerable success but the novelty of throwaway clothing never really caught on. It is not surprising then that Torres is looking into applications for Fabrican that reach far beyond the world of fashion. The material is sterile and therefore ideal for dressing wounds or acting as an agent for drop-release medicines administered directly through the skin. In the home Fabrican could be used to repair or customize old clothes, remove stains, or act as a protective coating on existing upholstery. Torres has also looked into the possibility of using Fabrican to create lightweight upholstery for aircraft or automobile interiors.

The matted material produced by the Fabrican spray closely resembles felt and can be made in any color. The product can be applied finely to provide a light, almost see-through coating, or liberally to create a thick, dense cloth. The prototype Fabrican garments created so far are beautifully messy. There are no neat edges or pressed seams. They're like textile graffiti. Torres describes the experience of wearing these garments as "like being naked" and compares them to a second skin. Fabrican is a celebration of spontaneity. It brings to mind those teenage kids who spray their hair pink or green in acts of rebellion that rinse out after only one wash. In a similar fashion, each Fabrican garment is designed to be used only once. The material is biodegradable and can be ripped off and trashed after use.

LEFT AND OPPOSITE THESE GARMENTS WERE CREATED BY SPRAYING THE PRESSURIZED FABRICAN LIQUID AT THE MODEL'S SKIN. THE LIQUID IS MADE UP OF TINY COTTON FIBERS THAT BIND TOGETHER ON IMPACT TO FORM A MATERIAL THAT CLOSELY RESEMBLES FELT. THE GARMENTS ARE TOTALLY DISPOSABLE AND ONCE FINISHED WITH CAN BE CLEANLY PEELED AWAY.

CHAPTER 2

BEHIND A PAINTED SMILE

The art of disguise is not just for Halloween parties and costume balls. Masks, prostheses, make-up, and camouflage are effective means of revealing our hidden natures anytime, anywhere. Dressing out of the ordinary is a liberating experience that scrambles established codes of age, gender, race, and class.

This chapter looks at scenarios where clothes and accessories are used as walls to hide behind or screens on which to project, so that individuals can adopt new personas and act and speak in ways they wouldn't dream of when wearing "regular" outfits. The attire in this chapter is intentionally out of step with conventional garb and is often used to subvert established orders or to transform identities.

Many of these artists, activists, scientists, performers, and fetishists use fashion in playful and ironic ways, as jesters or clowns do, to speak the truth or offer insight. Josh MacPhee's cut-out balaclava, for instance, or The Yes Men's clown-like *Management Leisure suit* address the controversial topics of terrorism and globalization, but in humorous ways. Behind the comic faces and funny suits are serious opinions that might otherwise be lambasted or ignored if delivered "straight." Likewise, Wolfgang Stehle's *social prosthesis* and Yuka Oyama's *wedding March* dress provoke meaningful questions about identity and gender through witty reworkings of traditional attire.

Masks also feature large here because, like hand puppets, they encourage depersonalization and enable their wearers to speak through the mouth of someone or something else. This ranges from the self-made costumes of Dungeon Majesty to the visual Kei make-up of Japanese teenage girls to the Victorian-era costumes of New York-based artists McDermott and McGough. Masking is also key to artist Krzysztof Wodiczko's *Dis-Armor* technological prothesis. Worn like a rucksack and rigged with rear-mounted LCD screens, the garment enables its wearer to speak with someone he or she fears without having to physically turn in their direction.

In many societies, not looking someone directly in the face has negative connotations. Nonetheless, the public is fascinated with people—from the Lone Ranger to bank robbers to Mexican wrestlers—who keep their identities to themselves. To hide an aspect of oneself is to leave much to the imagination of others and is therefore considered intriguing and even sexy. For some, the more a body is disguised and restricted by its costume, the more it becomes an object of desire and obsession. In turn-of-the-century Vienna, for example, high-heeled, lace-up boots that immobilized the feet and disabled the wearer from walking were a popular erotic fashion. similarly, the fantasy rubberwear of мercedes and Gen and нouse of нarlot limits the movement of the body so that others may admire and touch it. ɪn both cases, restriction also doubles as an experimental, if temporary, means of escaping the body's natural attributes.

Escapism is perhaps the reason why sorcerers, action heroes, and sci-fi characters also share a special place in the poplar imagination. тheir extraordinary powers set them apart from mere mortals and endow them with superstar status. тhe superhuman ability to disappear, for example, continues to fascinate and is now being taken up on a practical level by scientist susumu тachi. нis *optical camouflage* jacket uses projected images to soften its wearers' borders and help them blend into the environment. ɪllusionism and slight of hand are also a feature of the center for тactical мagic's *ultimate jacket* which is inspired by and contains as many secret pockets and compartments as may be found in the costumes of magicians.

тhose who dress out of sync with the present moment or veer from accepted standards of appearance are often considered suspicious and may be labeled weird, trashy, flaky, or, in some instances, insane. тhis chapter seeks to disprove the theory that different equals suspect by presenting a range of garments that play an important role in self-realization.

Emiya and Sasa are pictured hanging around a photo-me-booth in Harajuku, a famous shopping district in Tokyo. Sasa has made up her face to look as if she's been shot through the cheek. When the pair were asked to pose for a photo she pulled out a replica handgun and held it against her head.

Avid fans of Japan's visual kei music genre go to extreme lengths to dress like their favorite bands. Some followers, known as gothic Lolitas, dress like 19th century widowers in frilly black petticoats and lace bonnets, but all the girls pictured here have gone for more of a slasher-movie look. Visual bands first appeared on the Japanese underground in the late 1980s, playing a noisy fusion of thrash metal, Goth, punk, and glam rock. It wasn't so much the music that the bands were noted for but their appearance. Influenced by the likes of 1970s' rockers Alice Cooper, David Bowie, Kiss, and 1980s' New Romantics, the usually all-male visual groups sport overt theatrical make-up and elaborate, gender-bending costumes.

Most followers of visual kei are teenage girls. They tend to be attracted to bands including Pierrot, Kagrra, and Baroque by their looks as much as their sounds. The attention to detail that the fans pay to their own costumes is amazing. Many of them congregate around the photo-me booths to take pictures of their efforts. The two girls wearing red boiler suits are kitted out like street-savvy vampires. Their white face paint, dark lipstick, and heavy eye makeup gives them the look of sun-shy bloodsuckers, a style shared by Kyouhi, the girl in the black coat. In addition to making herself up to look like a vampire, Kyouhi has painted her face to look as though she's been slashed with a kitchen knife. Horror obviously has a major influence over the visual kei scene and just as a scary movie provides an hour and a half of frightful escapism, the dressing up associated with visual kei provides a bit of light—or rather dark—relief for inventive Japanese teenagers.

OPPOSITE THESE GIRLS HAVE THE BONNETS AND LACE POPULAR WITH FOLLOWERS OF THE GOTHIC LOLITA STYLE OF VISUAL KEI DRESS BUT HAVE RIPPED THEM TO SHREDS TO CREATE GARMENTS THAT RESEMBLE SLASHED-UP VICTORIAN STRAIGHT JACKETS.

LEFT, TOP AND BOTTOM
VAMPIRES, ZOMBIES, AND OTHER HORROR MOVIE STAPLES PROVIDE PLENTY OF INSPIRATION FOR FOLLOWERS OF JAPAN'S VISUAL KEI MUSIC SCENE. THE DUO IN RED BOILER SUITS ARE DRESSED LIKE URBAN VAMPIRES WHEREAS KYHOUI (FAR LEFT) AND EMIYA AND SASA (BELOW) ARE MADE UP WITH GRUESOME FACIAL INJURIES.

ultimate jacket, 2003

According to members of the center for tactical magic, the purpose of the *ultimate jacket* may be summed up in two words: autonomy and agency. concealing no less than fifty pockets and designed to hold a vast array of useful items for everyday interdiction, the *ultimate jacket* is at once stylish sportswear and inconspicous cover. made from abrasion-resistant, non-reflective, waterproof material and fully reversible with removable sleeves, it is, according to CTM, "the perfect complement for any tactical operation, emergency situation, or social occasion."

The jacket was the first official project to fully express the various tactics that the artists and activists who comprise CTM advocate: surprise, infiltration, subterfuge, disguise, misdirection, sabotage, stealth, evasion, and surveillance. As CTM explain, the jacket "empowers the wearer to become the site of action, intervention, and performance. It is a self-contained unit capable of responding to any condition at a moment's notice…and is perhaps the most appropriate costume for staging events in a theater of conflict. It changes shape (sleeves come off), color (it's reversible) and purpose (depending on wearer and pocketed items)."

The inspiration for the jacket came from working with a magician, a private detective, and a ninja. "Upon realizing that all three of them were using secret pockets—the magician for tricks, the P.I. for surveillance devices, and the ninja for weapons and distraction devices," says CTM member Aaron Gach, "it just seemed to make sense that all good activists, interventionists, and mischief-makers should have secret pockets also." To date, the jacket has gone through three separate prototype stages but the CTM hope to have a relatively affordable production model within a year. "This would be ideal," says Gach, "since the jacket is meant be worn and activated in social space. We've had many requests in this regard."

Recently CTM teamed up artist Basia Irland

"Absolutely, Positively, the BEST ★★★★★ Tactical Duty Gear EVER."

ULTIMATE

The ULTIMATE JACKET
50 Secret Pockets, Endless Possibilities

1) Ninja style mask is quickly removed from collar pocket and; 2) can be worn to conceal identity 3) Disposable latex gloves are retrieved from outer sleeve pocket 4) Gloves should be worn prior to infiltration to prevent fingerprinting. 5) Entering the inner sleeve pocket; 6) provides access to a high-intensity, low visibility red light to assist in seeing without being seen 7) Procured documents slip easily into large back pocket

to redesign the water sampling gear of aquatic biologist Kari Burr of the environmental advocacy group Deltakeepers. Together with Irland, CTM produced a variation of the *ultimate jacket* that resembles a fishing vest and contains compartments for the various items used to test water quality. Prior to the new togs, Kari was forced to haul her gear around in a large plastic crate. Now everything is within hand's reach, neatly sorted into different pockets, well-protected, and accessible; plus, the weight is evenly distributed throughout the garment so that it doesn't feel heavy or bulky and is easy to move around in. In both its manifestations, the *ultimate jacket* facilitates a variety of actions for its wearer and is a testimony to the positive social applications of tactical and magical thinking.

FAR LEFT THE *ULTIMATE JACKET DISPLAY* WAS INITIALLY CREATED FOR "THE INTERVENTIONISTS" EXHIBITION AT THE MASSACHUSETTS MUSEUM OF CONTEMPORARY ART. AS VISITORS APPROACHED, THE LIFE-SIZED ACTION FIGURE BEGAN TO ROTATE ON A REVOLVING MANHOLE COVER. LIGHTS BEHIND A FAUX STOREFRONT FLICKERED AND A TV CHANNEL-SURFED BETWEEN FOUND FOOTAGE AND AN *ULTIMATE JACKET* INFOMERCIAL.

LEFT AND OPPOSITE THE DESIGN OF THE *ULTIMATE JACKET* MAKES REFERENCE TO MARTIAL ARTS AND MILITARY UNIFORMS, THE POCKETED SUITS OF MAGICIAN AND PRIVATE DETECTIVES, AS WELL AS UTILITY JACKETS, BOTH MILITARY AND CIVILIAN.

THE ULTIMATE JACKET

Firepaw   **Lucky Strike**   **Air-Vantage**

Fifty Secret Pockets Endless Possibilities !

CENTER FOR TACTICAL MAG

Surprise   Infiltration   Subterfuge

Evasion   Stealth   Sabotage

Surveillance   Misdirection   Disguise

wedding march, 2001

wedding march is the name of a performance by artist Yuka Oyama that took place in Munich, Germany in the summer of 2001. For a mock journey to the altar, Oyama designed and handcrafted a very unusual wedding gown and veil. Both pieces were made from multiple, plastic sandbags which were suspended by industrial strength hooks from a padded metal belt and headpiece worn by Oyama in her role as "bride." In total, the dress and veil weighed over 170 pounds. For the performance, Oyama proceeded alone towards the city's wedding hall among other couples waiting to tie the knot. Because the dress and veil were so heavy—and each bag had to be moved individually by hand—her march to the altar was a long, tedious drag that lasted nearly three hours, during which 15 other couples were married.

"I was 26 when I made this work. It is the age that is known to be the 'prime time' to get married in Japan," says Oyama, who is of Japanese descent. "It is also said that if you miss this timing you will be left alone, single forever. There is a saying that an unmarried woman older than this age is like 'a day-old christmas cake.'"

In 1840, English girl-bride Queen Victoria wore a white wedding gown to marry Prince Albert. It was a fashion statement that changed the western world's thinking about what brides should look like since until that time most women wore their best dresses of any color when they got married. With the Victorian Age, white came to symbolize purity and became the symbolic color of weddings—a standard that prevails today.

Oyama's wedding dress critiques both Eastern and Western ideals by substituting whispery whites with heavy metal and shiny plastic that is as much under construction as it is restrictive. At the time Oyama made the dress, many of her friends had already made the leap. But for Oyama, defining her own understanding of "commitment in marriage, becoming a wife, and doing what one is supposed to do at a certain age" resulted in a "heaviness in my head, slow, and struggling." *wedding march* provided a much-needed escape valve and material means of rebellion. Moreover, the wedding finery poked fun at the vision-in-white stereotype perpetuated by the factory wedding and emphasized "the empty side in highly automated and commercialized contemporary wedding ceremonies."

LEFT AND OPPOSITE ARTIST YUKA OYAMA MAKES A LONG TRUDGE TO THE WEDDING BUREAU IN MUNICH OUTFITTED IN A 170-POUND GOWN MADE OF SANDBAGS. THE DRESS HARKS BACK TO THE VICTORIAN ERA, WHEN TIGHT CORSETS, LAYERED PETTICOATS, AND HEAVY BROCADE LOADED WOMEN DOWN AND SEVERLY RESTRICTED THEIR MOVEMENT. RATHER THAN REAFFIRM THE VICTORIAN STEREOTYPE, HOWEVER, OYAMA'S *WEDDING MARCH* DEMONSTRATES THAT SHE IS CAPABLE OF PULLING HER OWN WEIGHT.

camouflage clothing has until recently relied on the strategic use of color and disruptive patterns to conceal the person wearing it. Professor Susumu Tachi and his team at Tachi Lab, Tokyo University, have invented a cloak that appears to be transparent.

The "invisibility cloak" is actually a screen. Images are shot by a camera placed directly behind the subject, relayed through a computer, and then projected on to the front of the coat. Ordinarily this process would not be possible in broad daylight, as the projected image is not bright enough to be noticeable. Tachi's cloak is made using retro-reflective material, the same type of material applied to road signs and bicycle reflectors. When light is projected on to a non-retro-reflective surface, such as a cinema screen, it bounces off in all directions. When an image is projected on to a retro-reflective surface, such as Tachi's cloak, the light bounces back only in the direction from which it came. This means that the projected image is bright and clearly visible, even in daylight. Optical camouflage is still in the early stages of development, but Tachi hopes to apply the technology to scenarios where it would prove useful to "see through" a solid object, for instance the interior of a car or truck when trying to park, or the floor of an airplane cockpit when approaching a runway.

It would appear that in its current state the technology behind optical camouflage is probably best suited to situations where the position of the camera, projector, and projection surface are fixed rather than where a garment is in constant motion. In the near future, however, with the development of smart fabrics that behave like LCD screens, our clothes might be used to carry all kinds of images. Digital cameras are so small nowadays that they could easily be attached to the back of a coat. If the front of the coat were made from the LCD-like fabric then images taken with the camera could be fed into the screen at the front of the coat and render it invisible without the need for a projector. The whole system would be contained within the fabric of the coat.

Face corsets, 2002–2004

Paddy Hartley created his grotesque series of face corsets as an impermanent method of reshaping the human face. The face corsets are made up of reinforced panels of fabric that are hooked and laced together just like a corset for the body. As the laces are tightened, the fabric panels squeeze against the soft skin of the face and grossly distort the features. Different levels of distortion can be achieved by pulling tighter on the laces or changing the sequence in which they are fastened.

Hartley has long been fascinated by the many tortuous procedures, such as cosmetic surgery and anabolic steroid treatments, that people have endured in order to transform their appearance. "I became interested in exploring alternative ways of altering the face," stated the artist, "as if plastic surgery was taboo or had never been invented." Hartley began looking into the history of fashion and in particular the use of corsets as tools to manipulate the body, which prompted him to create his first corset for the face.

The project began in 2002 when Hartley was invited by the Victoria and Albert Museum in London to create a piece of work for an event that explored contemporary perceptions of cosmetic surgery. It was through this event that Hartley met Dr Ian Thompson, a biomaterials research scientist at the Department of Oral Maxillofacial Surgery in Guy's Hospital, London. Part of Thompson's work involves the surgical repair of facial injuries. This proved to be a source of fascination for Hartley and Thompson, likewise, was intrigued by Hartley's artwork. The pair established a collaborative working relationship and were awarded a grant from the Wellcome Trust to develop the face corset project further.

The first face corsets were made with white cotton drill and transparent PVC. The artist found that the material he used needed to be very strong so it wouldn't buckle or twist when tightly fastened. Cotton drill proved ideal and was also relatively easy to work with. The transparent PVC corsets look much more disturbing than the softer cotton versions. They are hard, they exaggerate the mutations of the face even further and can be very painful to wear. Hartley continued to experiment with different materials in later examples of the face corsets. Some are made with grey pinstripe and have the look of a business executive's suit. Others refer to specific periods in fashion history such as the soft pink face corset that has fastenings to match those of the 1940s. Hartley has also experimented with his own printed patterns on face corsets emblazoned with arrows and instructions to "pull" written around the eyelets.

Although Hartley is keen to stress the experimental nature of the face corsets, his working relationship with Dr Thompson has resulted in a practical application for the garments. A patient of Thompson's required external support below her lower lip after her bottom jawbone disintegrated. A transparent face corset seemed the perfect solution and one was made to remedy the problem.

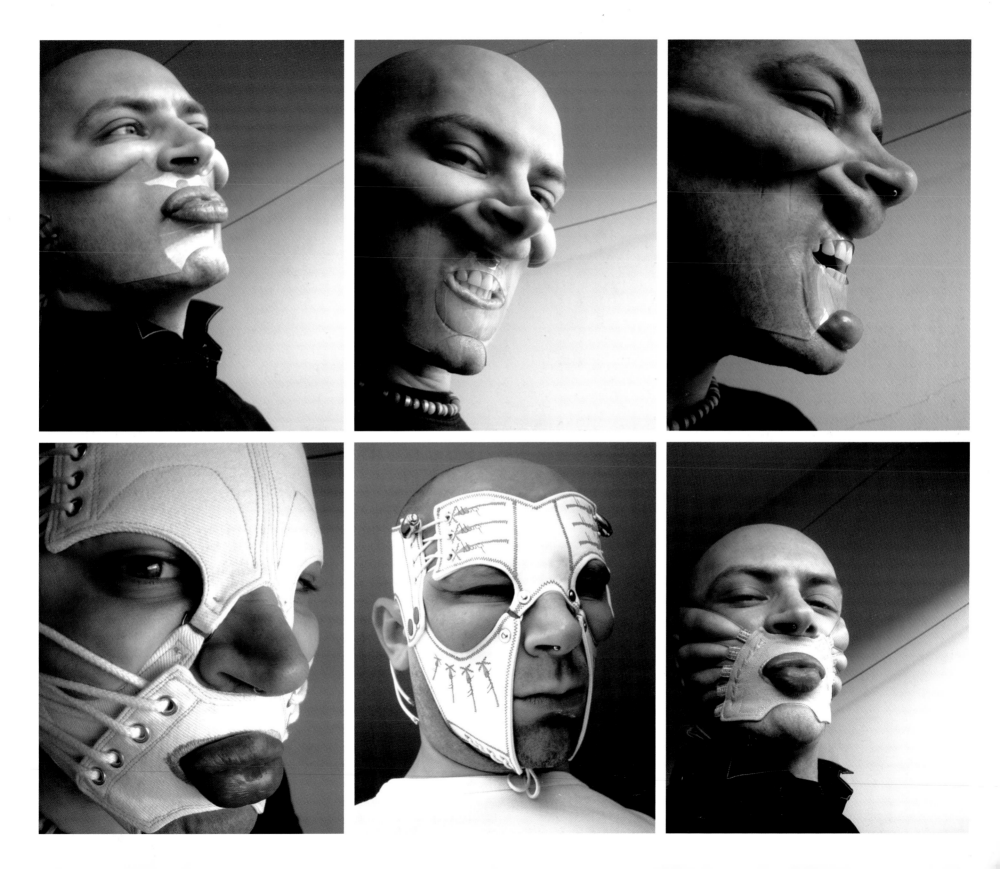

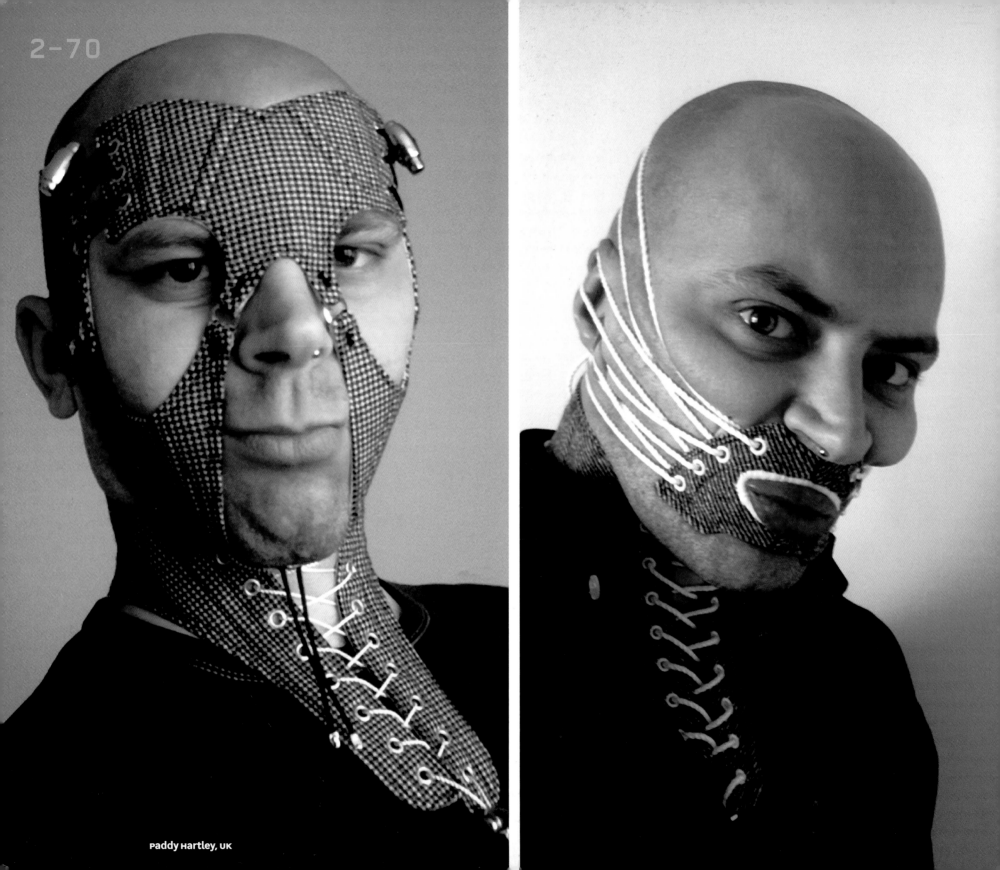

paddy hartley, uk

Alien Queen
Gerda Series
Star Pilots
Secret Agent

House of Harlot is a London-based fetish couturier founded in 1991 by Robin and Michelle Archer. The company is recognized worldwide for its provocative latex-rubber clothing designs. In addition to its own range of exotic fetish wear the company has also worked closely on collections for designers including Thierry Mugler and John Galliano. A further, vital part of the studio's creative output comes in the form of commissions from private clients and among its most illustrious are Mercedes and Gen.

"Gen" began designing extraordinary costumes for his wife, "Mercedes," in the early 1990s. Initially the costumes were made purely for their own amusement. Mercedes enjoys dressing up and modeling the garments, whereas Gen prefers to concentrate on designing and photographing them. He also has costumes of his own but doesn't enjoy dressing up as much as his wife. "Mercedes was very excited by the costumes," explains Gen. "When we discovered latex she also found she enjoyed wearing it, so it became a mutually fun thing to do."

Robin Archer and House of Harlot first came to the attention of Mercedes and Gen via an elaborate outfit called the *wasp,* which Archer created for his wife, Michelle. They embarked on a stimulating working relationship that thrives on close collaboration. Mercedes and Gen are always pushing the design of their costumes to make them ever more intricate—some are almost impossible to make. "There are very few people who can translate my ideas into a pattern," says Gen, adding, "Robin is a fantastic pattern-maker."

Interest in the costumes grew as the size of the couple's collection increased. As a result they created the "Mercedes and Gen" persona

for appearances at fetish events and the famous carnival in Venice. It was during a stay in Venice that Gen had the idea for the first *Gerda* costume. "We were due to take a launch to one of the islands in the Lagoon," he recalls. "The night before I had a very vivid dream about the story of Gerda, a story by Jim E. Dickson (thought to be a pseudonym of cult fetish writer and Atomage publisher John Sutcliff." The story revolves around Gerda, the most beautiful model in Paris. A dashing count persuades her to stay with him on his secluded Mediterranean island. On the boat journey there he dresses her in a rubber outfit to protect her from the splashing waves. Gen imagined every detail of this outfit in his dream and sketched it on a napkin the next morning. Archer was staying with Gen at the time and immediately wanted to realize the costume. It is composed of layer upon layer of ghostly white latex fitted and decorated with an incredible array of detail.

Mercedes and Gen have accumulated over 30 costumes in the ten years they've been pursuing their extraordinary passion, but not all of them are made by Archer. Recently Gen has started modeling computer-generated scenes that act as backdrops for his photographs of Mercedes. This returns the costumes to the realm of fantasy and completes the cycle started by the first sketches.

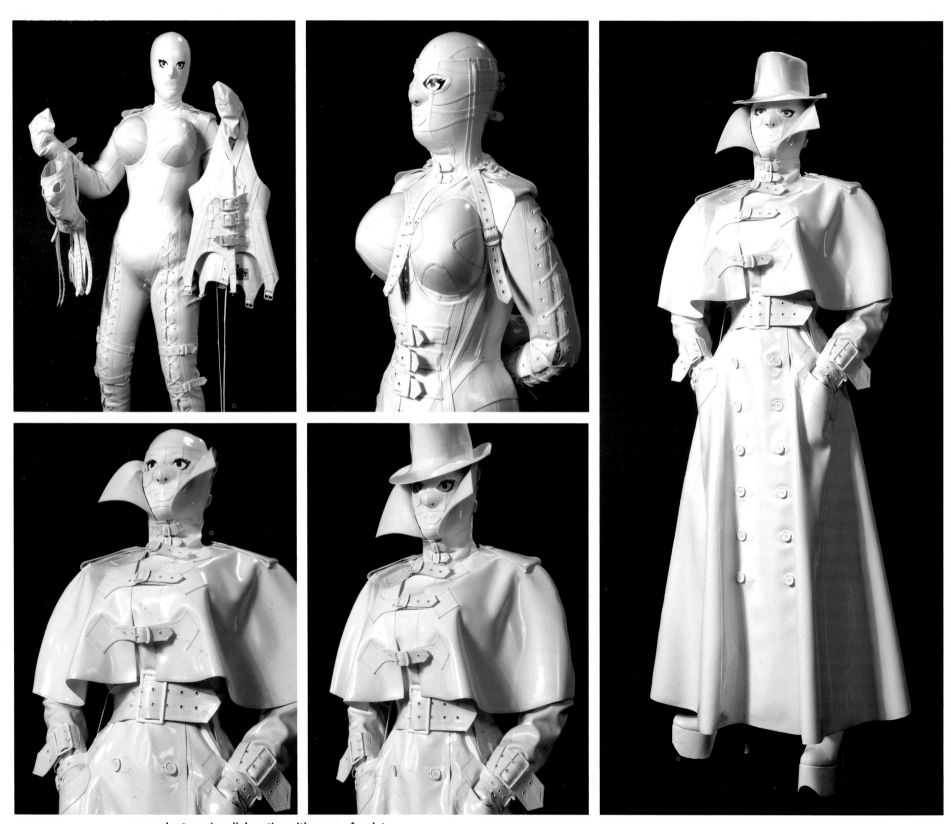

mercedes & ɢen in collaboration with ʜouse of ʜarlot

JOSH MACPHEE, USA

The Mask Project: Terrorism Begins at Home, 2003 & ongoing

THIS PAGE AND OPPOSITE

ARTIST JOSH MACPHEE HAS BEEN INTERESTED IN THE PUBLIC APPLICATION OF MASKS FOR SOME TIME. FOR A RECENT ART PROJECT, HE CREATED MASKS WHICH COULD BE COPIED ONTO STICKER PAPER, CUT OUT, AND APPLIED TO THE FACES OF POLITICIANS, CELEBRITIES, AND MODELS ON MAGAZINE COVERS, POSTERS, AND BILLBOARDS, SUCH AS ROLLING STONE MAGAZINE AND IKEA, SEEN HERE.

For a number of years now, chicago-based artist Josh MacPhee has been experimenting with various ways of integrating the art of disguise into everyday life, often through sketches of business people wearing masks or by painting masked figures on the street. on the occasion of an art project called *copy cat,* MacPhee received the opportunity to test out some of his ideas in public.

Intended to promote the free flow of art and information, *copy cat* was organized by chicago-based artist Brett Bloom and writer Lars Bang Larsen for the Aarhus Art Academy in Denmark in October 2003. over 60 artists, activists, and collaborators from diverse backgrounds were invited to produce a work that could be easily reproduced, dispersed, and reinterpreted by a broad public. The goal was to make something that could be fully implemented only when photocopied and distributed by viewers/users. MacPhee's contribution, *the Mask Project: Terrorism Begins at Home,* consisted of drawings of ski masks that people could copy onto sticker paper and, if they so desired, place over the faces of people in corporate advertisements.

Masks, like slogan-covered T-shirts, are an effective and clear means of expressing moods and sentiments. The ski mask, in particular, is a potent conveyor of meaning because of its association with extremists and hi-jackers. In the US, where free speech has recently come under limits, MacPhee's masks have played an important role in helping the general public to voice their opinions without repercussion (so long as they don't get caught at the scene).

Depending on who applied the masks and to whom, the resulting message varied from humorous to surreal to appropriate. one cheeky participant applied the face mask to the mug of a serene young family man in an IKEA advertisement—a revealing statement on the banal, home-grown roots of some of the spectacular acts of terrorism that we see on television.

Conservative politicians in the US like to remind us that we are never safe, as well as to illustrate this fact with pictures of evil-doers in balaclavas. However, MacPhee's masks point the finger back in the direction of the Homeland to question their role in the problem. "I use the phrase because it references the 'safety Begins at Home' materials that I remember from grade school that told us what to do in case of a fire and that you should always lock your doors, never talk to strangers, etc.," says MacPhee.

The masks from the *copy cat* project have shown up in a number of cities around the United States but since they are part of a guerrilla project, it has been difficult to know exactly where the actions of the general public leave off and the reactions of the government begin. "For me, masks placed in advertising play with and raise questions about the relationship of capitalism to fear, safety, anonymity, guerrilla activity, and terror," says MacPhee. However, "cities in the united states are becoming obsessed with the removal of any form of expression that is not state- or corporate-sponsored, so most masks don't last more than 24 to 48 hours."

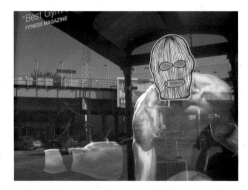

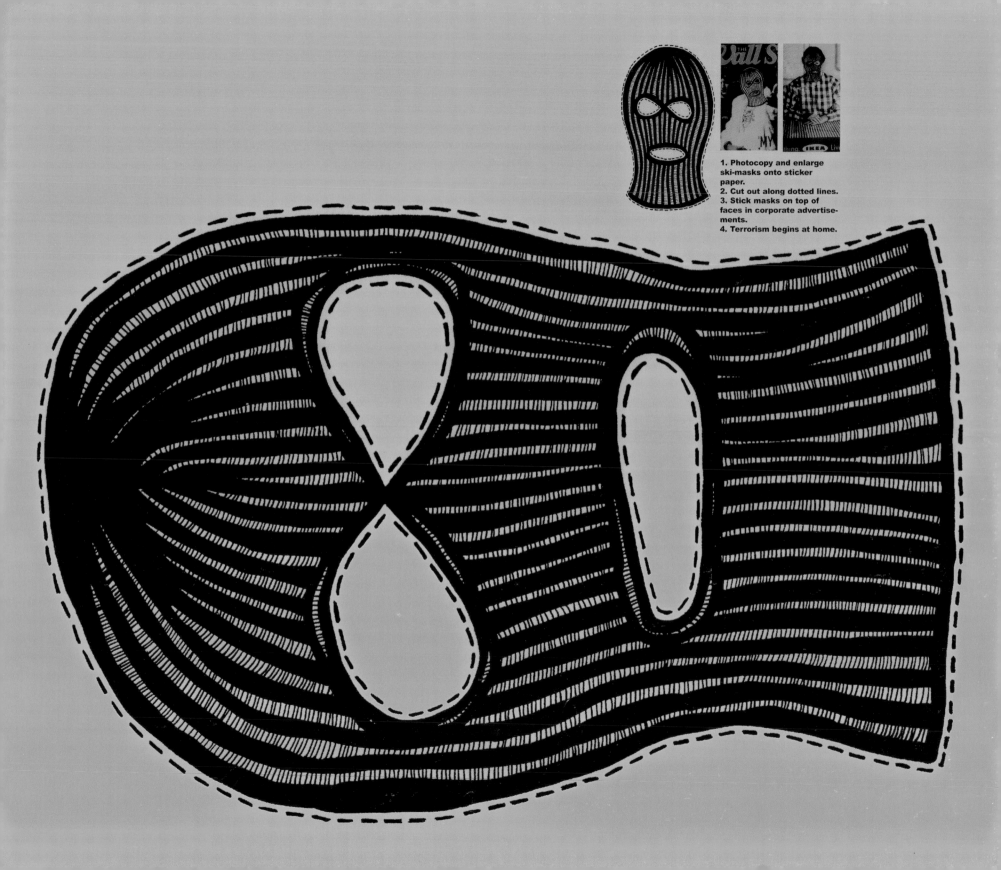

1. Photocopy and enlarge ski-masks onto sticker paper.
2. Cut out along dotted lines.
3. Stick masks on top of faces in corporate advertisements.
4. Terrorism begins at home.

WOLFGANG STEHLE, GERMANY

social prosthesis, 2000

Drinking together is a form of complicity, a sign of camaraderie, goodwill, loyalty, and trust. It is such a time-honored tradition that the individual who does not join in is looked upon with amazement and even suspicion. Drinking is also a manly thing to do and the possessor of a robust beer belly is often characterized as a jovial, amiable type. In certain macho contexts, men who don't drink are even considered effeminate.

Munich-based artist Wolfgang Stehle does not drink, but he has attempted to counterbalance the perceived social inadequacy by creating a prototype alcohol-intake system that may be worn over or under one's existing clothes. The apparatus is a gumball-pink, plastic prosthesis that was molded, cast, and finished by hand. It curves over the shoulders and features a long esophagus that ends in a perfectly swollen, mannered stomach. Beverages are poured into an opening at the device's top and make their way down a hollow throat into a belly that holds up to ten liters of alcohol or other liquid. When in use, the surrogate tummy enables Stehle or other users to "drink" with friends at social gatherings, and to hang out with the men while using the lavatory, thanks to a small valve at the base of the stomach that opens and closes like a mechanical urethra.

The device was born of Stehle's memories of his own struggle to fit in as a teenager and addresses the ongoing dilemma of non-drinkers. For him it seemed only natural to counteract feelings of inadequacy by creating a device that could substitute for bodily and social functions that were missing (at least from the perspective of others). It is therefore no surprise that his creation is a monster of sorts that conjurs up all kinds of associations and mixed emotions. The prothesis looks like a prop from a David Cronenberg film and clings to it wearer's body like a needy child, a deformed twin, or an ill-fitting brace, pushing the limits of "fitting in" to absurd levels. It also gives Stehle the rather frumpy and amusing appearance of being pregnant. Above all, it critiques the ridiculous lengths we will pursue to be accepted by others by offering a highly personal and cheeky alternative to the norm.

ABOVE AND RIGHT MADE OF CANDY-COLORED PLASTIC, ARTIST WOLFGANG STEHLE'S *SOCIAL PROTHESIS* IS A PROTOTYPE BELLY FOR NON-DRINKERS. ALCOHOLIC BEVERAGES ARE POURED INTO A "MOUTH" AT THE TOP AND STORED IN THE STOMACH UNTIL A TRIP TO THE LOO IS NECESSARY.

OPPOSITE IN MANY SOCIETIES, NON-DRINKERS ARE OFTEN VIEWED WITH SUSPICION AND FIND THEMSELVES IN THE AWKWARD POSITION OF HAVING TO APOLOGIZE FOR NOT CONSUMING. STEHLE'S DEVICE KEEPS HIM FROM UPSETTING THE STATUS QUO BY ALLOWING HIM TO GO WITH THE FLOW.

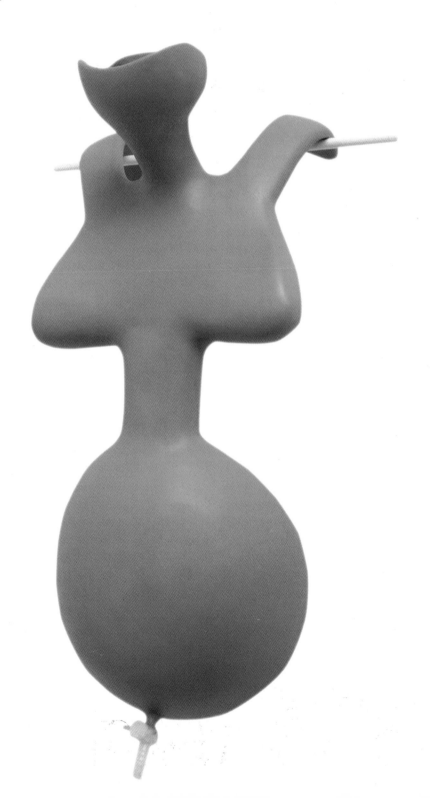

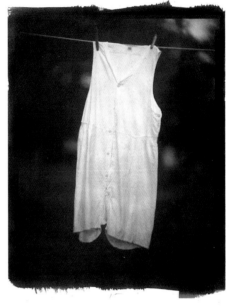

THIS PAGE AND OPPOSITE DELIBERATELY LOOKING BACKWARDS FOR THEIR FASHION CUES, ARTISTS MCDERMOTT AND MCGOUGH BORROW FROM THE MODES, MANNERS, AND PRESENTATION OF THE EARLY 20TH-CENTURY DANDY. KEY GARMENTS IN EACH ARTIST'S WARDROBE ARE PICTURED HERE, INCLUDING TOP HATS, TAILS, AND STIFF COLLARS.

LEFT TO RIGHT *A MEANS OF IDENTIFYING THE WEARER*, 1911/1991. PALLADIUM PRINT, 112 X 14 IN. *THE HAT AMBRY*, 1907/1989. CYANOTYPE, 10 X 8 IN. *WHOSE BRIGHTEST THREADS ARE EACH A WASTED DAY*, 1923/1992. PALLADIUM PRINT, 14 X 11 IN.

OPPOSITE CLOCKWISE FROM TOP LEFT *PORTRAIT OF THE ARTISTS (WITH TOP HATS)*, 1865/1991. PALLADIUM PRINT, 14 X 11 IN. *LES INCROYABLES*, 1893/1989. CYANOTYPE, 10 X 8 IN. *PORTRAIT OF THE ARTIST WITH HIS SPILL VASES*, 1907/1989. CYANOTYPE, 10 X 9 IN.

clothing is a potent sign of the times. when it is out of step with the present, it sends a particularly strong message to others that its wearers don't want to be reminded of the here and now. Indeed, clothing is the ultimate time machine. It survives decades and even centuries after its users have gone and perpetuates over time the mores of another era. Fabric, color, cut, and even the way in which garments are fastened and attached to the body all play significant roles in expressing a society's social habits at a particular moment. For artists David McDermott and Peter McGough, outmoded fashion was the perfect escape hatch.

Formerly a couple living in New York and Dublin, McDermott and McGough chose to consciously divorce themselves from the manners and modes of the present day by living in the style of 20th-century dandies. Their home had no electricity or modern plumbing. They drove a 1914 Roadster. Above all, they were never seen in anything but the fashions of a hundred years ago: top hats,

bowlers, stiff collars, knickers, tweeds, fur coats, gloves, and spats. The pair were anachronistically anarchistic.

The two met in the New York vaudeville scene of the 1980s and continue to use their Oscar Wilde eccentricity as the springboard for their work: homoerotic films, paintings, and photographs that hark back to the early years of the 20th century. Romantic, spiritual, mystical, and campy, their art represents an idyllic, simpler time that has never really existed but continues to be a source of hope and happiness for those wishing to escape the banality of the modern world.

The idea for their identity change came from a turn-of-the-century book they found that provided instruction on how a young man should live his life, how he should behave, and how he could become a successful and prominent figure. They decided to follow the book's advice in full and haven't looked back since. After the switch it was not possible to distinguish their way of living from the work they produced and vice versa. This is perhaps

because their personal and artistic style was influenced by the Victorian and Edwardian periods, during which art and life were more fully integrated than they are today.

Although it is not unusual for artists to invoke the past, McDermott and McGough meticulously rebuilt it. To them, their dress and manners were not pretend or fictitious but belonged to a real-time continuum they created and that allowed them to get on with contemporary life in a way that would not be possible sans old-world finery.

Breakaway Business suit, 2001
Management Leisure suit, 2001

The Yes Men are a group of individual activists whose number is indefinite and fluid. According to their website, a person becomes a Yes Man "by exposing, perhaps deviously, the nastiness of powerful evildoers", although the identities of the group's members remain, for the most part, undercover. At the moment, the activities of The Yes Men are associated with their two most visible members, Mike Bonanno and Andy Bichlbaum.

The Yes Men employ the age-old strategy of satire to expose the flaws of their right-wing opponents. In 1999, for instance, they developed a website titled www.GATT.org that parodied the language and policies of the World Trade Organization. The website was so thorough in its mimicry that many people believed it to be the official site for the General Agreement on Tariffs and Trade. The mix-up is precisely what the Yes Men had anticipated, but they didn't predict that visitors to the site would invite them to make television appearances and give lectures at universities and business conventions on behalf of the WTO.

The *Breakaway Business suit* and *Manage-*

ment Leisure suit are remnants of one of The Yes Men's most memorable and humorous attempts to get experts to notice they weren't WTO representatives. In January 2001, the organizers of a "Textiles of the Future" conference in Tampere, Finland sent an email to GATT.org asking for a WTO representative to deliver the keynote address. For the occasion, Bonanno and Bichlbaum called upon their good friend and costumer to the stars, Sal Salamone, to design a special outfit.

Dressed in a seemingly normal business suit and posing as Hank Hardy Unruh, Bichlbaum held forth on the history of the textile industry, claiming, among other things, that the US civil war, fought over cotton, was a waste of money because slavery would eventually be replaced by the sweatshops of today. He went on to characterize Gandhi's spin-your-own-clothes revolts as naïve, and opined that the British could have taken advantage of the situation by incorporating homespun garments into their production lines. Strangely, none of the delegates objected to the outrageous claims.

The real element of surprise came at the

conclusion to the talk when Bichlbaum's business suit (*Breakaway Business suit*) was ripped open to reveal a gold, stretch-nylon bodysuit (*Management Leisure suit*) rigged with a three-foot-long "Employee visualization Appendage." The fabric member was equipped with a so-called video interface meant to enable managers to watch their workers in remote locations and give them electric shocks if necessary.

In this instance, it was only through extreme fashion that a reaction could be achieved. As Mike Bonanno recently noted in *The Guardian*: "That's what's amazing about the discourse in this country. People are so used to complete absurdity that nothing surprises them anymore."

LEFT A REFINED VERSION OF THE *MANAGEMENT LEISURE SUIT* WITH ANATOMICALLY CORRECT BODY PARTS.

OPPOSITE ANDY BICHLBAUM OF THE YES MEN, POSING AS HANK HARDY UNRUH FROM THE WORLD TRADE ORGANIZATION, APPROACHING THE FINALE TO HIS SATIRIC LECTURE AT A "TEXTILES OF THE FUTURE" CONFERENCE IN TAMPERE, FINLAND, 2001. AS UNRUH'S SPEECH COMES TO A CLOSE, FELLOW CONSPIRATOR MIKE BONNANO SURPRISES AUDIENCE MEMBERS BY STRIPPING UNRUH OF HIS *BREAKAWAY BUSINESS SUIT* TO REVEAL A GOLDEN *MANAGE-MENT LEISURE SUIT* AND PHALLUS-LIKE "EMPLOYEE VISUALIZATION APPENDAGE" BENEATH.

Dis-Armor, 2004

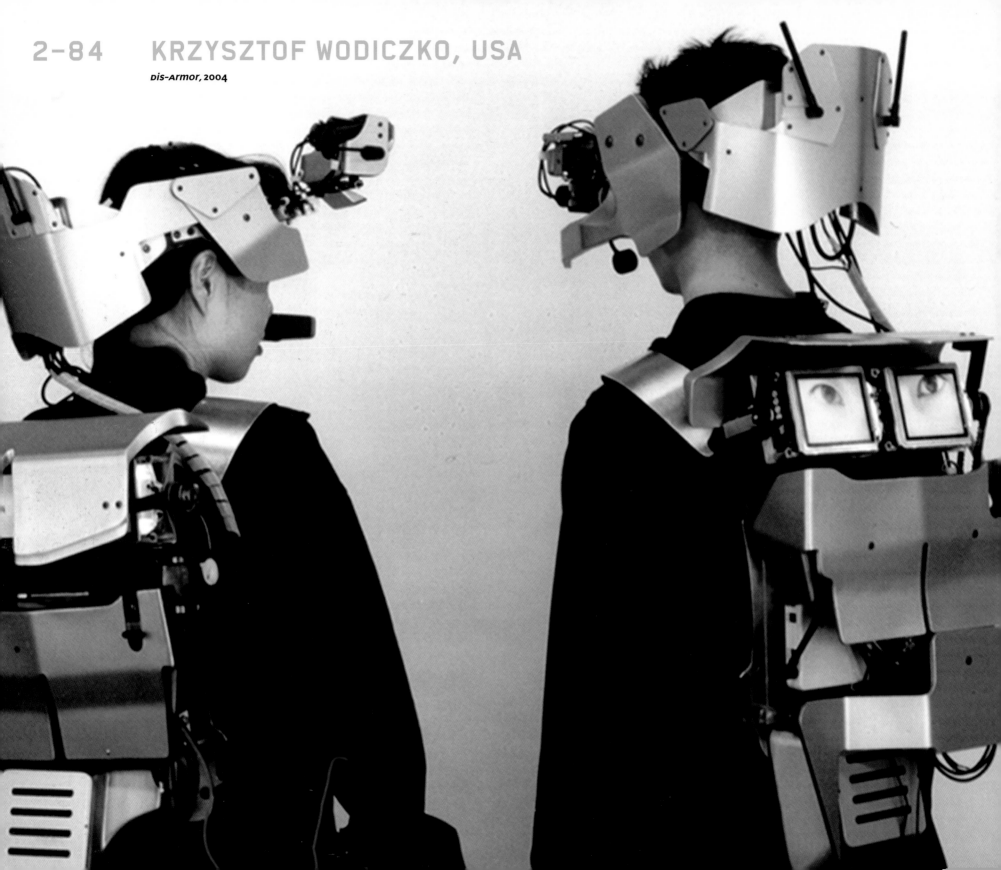

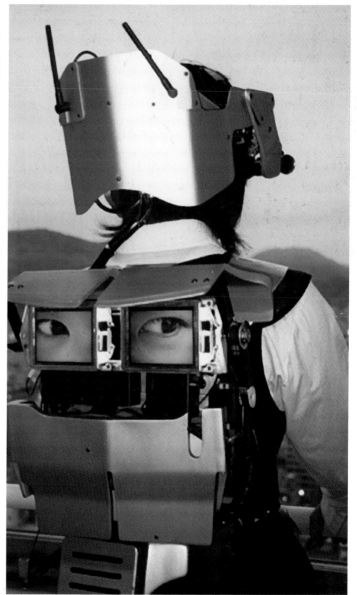

Artist Krzysztof Wodiczko has a long-standing reputation for combining architecture, industrial design, and the visual arts into objects that address conditions of alienation, cultural isolation, and disenfranchisement. *Dis-Armor* is the most recent in a series of wearable prosthetic communication equipment designed to assist neglected, abused, or otherwise marginalized persons— often immigrants and troubled youths— residing in today's cities. Victims suffering from social or physical duress often find it difficult to express their feelings and experiences through face-to-face discourse. *Dis-Armor* provides an indirect means of breaking the silence. A combination of helmet and backpack, the portable device frees people to speak their minds by enabling them to talk to each other's backs.

Media plays a central role in creating a dialogue. Inside the wearer's helmet are cameras that capture and transmit live images of the user's eyes to a pair of liquid crystal display screens mounted on his or her back. Below the LCD screens is a speaker that amplifies the user's voice to the person behind. Also attached to the wearer's helmet are a rearview mirror and video camera, as well as a monitor, microphone, and headphone which enable the user to see and hear the person standing behind them. Although the outward "face" of the user takes on the qualities of a robot or television to the person behind, the gear is an effective alternative means—in a playful R2D2 kind of way—for the user to address people and topics they normally could not or would not.

Originally created for the Hiroshima City Museum of Contemporary Art, with shy or intorverted Japanese high school students in mind, the device has also been used to assist Arab-Americans discuss their experiences post-September 11 as part of *The Interventionists* exhibition at the Massachusetts Museum of Contemporary Art in North Adams, Pennsylvania. As it names suggests, *Dis-Armor* is a protective suit that helps persons in weak positions lay down their arms, drop their guard, and be themselves.

Dungeon Majesty, 2004

BELOW THE DUNGEONMASTER (AKA RILEY SWIFT) IS THE OMNIPOTENT POWER THAT CONTROLS THE GAME AND ALL THE MONSTERS THE TEAM ENCOUNTER.

FOLLOWING PAGES (FROM LEFT TO RIGHT) SHAKUNTALA IS A DRUID PLAYED BY SARAH LOW AND HER BEST WEAPON IS THE SCIMITAR, BUT SHE CAN ALSO SPEAK WITH ANIMALS. MYSTIKA IS A CLERIC PLAYED BY JENNIFER JUNIPER STRATFORD AND HER BEST WEAPON IS THE MACE, BUT SHE ALSO ACTS AS THE TEAM'S HEALER. LATIZA IS AN ELVIN SORCERESS PLAYED BY LIZA CARDINALE AND HER BEST WEAPON IS THE MAGIC MISSILE. AND FINALLY, DEVASTINA IS A HUMAN BARBARIAN PLAYED BY CHRISTINE IVANOW AND HER BEST WEAPON IS THE GREAT AXE.

Dressing up is a great way of escaping the humdrum routine of everyday life. Some like to spend their weekends dressed up as cowboys, soldiers, or even Elvis Presley, but this group of girlfriends from Hollywood, California, love to dress as warriors from the fantasy adventure game Dungeons and Dragons.

It all started when the girls, Liza Cardinale, Christine Ivanow, Sarah Low, and, Jennifer Juniper Stratford, were introduced to D&D by a visiting friend who was a Dungeonmaster (the player who controls the game). They were hooked but unfortunately he had to leave town and the girls were left in desperate need of someone to takeover the game. "Sometimes it's embarrassing to admit you play D&D," says Stratford (aka Mystika), so she was really made up to discover that Riley Swift, a colleague at her workplace, was a fan of the game, and not only that, he was also a Dungeonmaster looking for new friends to play with. Stratford invited him over to meet the others and they've been playing together ever since.

Around the same time the four girlfriends were developing ideas for a public access TV show. They decided to make a show about adventure, fantasy, and their all-time favorite game, which they called Dungeon Majesty. In the show the game is played out in real time in the studio with all the participants dressed in jeans and customized T-shirts. The studio-based material is then mixed in post-production with footage of the gang dressed as their fantasy characters battling with animated monsters. All the players are involved in every aspect of the show and in designing and making the costumes, which are as wild as the characters they play. Latiza, for instance, is an Elvin sorceress who also dishes out advice to viewers by consulting the oracle Monkelonda (a pug dog who appears in a magic mirror dressed in a wig and a cloak). There's also Devastina, a recently literate Barbarian who reviews romance novels in a slot titled Devastina's Dungeon Diaries.

Dungeons and Dragons is mostly thought of as a game for nerdy adolescent boys, and some members of the gaming community assume that Dungeon Majesty must be a spoof because they doubt that girls actually play. Cardinale, Ivanow, Low, Stratford, and Swift obviously love playing the game, but the opportunity to dress up in fantastic outfits and battle strange beasts also has a big appeal.

dungeon majesty, usa

CHAPTER 3

TO PROTECT AND TO SERVE

conventional clothes just hang around but purpose-built garments work for you. why pack, strap, or attach survival equipment onto your body? clothing is its own portable environment that extends the body's functions and is an active second skin.

Rather than focusing on the law-and-order utility wear of police uniforms, biohazard suits, and paramilitary gear, the chapter "To Protect and To Serve" features multifunctional attire that pushes the boundaries of what is considered clothing *per se*. The garments herein are designed to protect or serve the bodies of their individual users by assisting their movements, guarding their peripheries, enhancing their functions, or extending their physical spaces.

Here we delve into the realm of body coverings that move limbs, send electrical shocks, deflect bullets, ward off animal attacks, or insulate against extreme temperatures. Also considered are moldable, modular, inflatable, and otherwise transformable garments that allow their wearers to reshape their space, take up more "room," and achieve a great deal of mobility in the process.

Key to this chapter is the fact that we no longer inhabit an industrial landscape but a service society, a condition reflected in the expectations we have for our clothing. It is not enough that our garments are well-made or practical; they should perform and provide for us as well. It would be great if robots could take over our tasks for us, as reflected in recent films such as *Artificial Intelligence* and *I, Robot*. Until they do, Japan-based scientist Yoshiyuki Sankai is bringing us one step closer to this reality with *HAL-3*, a hybrid assistive limb, that does the walking for you. Developed foremostly for persons with "gait disorder" or weak leg muscles in mind, the company aims to develop a model which will allow users to run as fast as Olympic athletes in the future.

High-tech clothing that contributes to self-sufficiency and self-confidence is also being explored by artists, fashion designers, and commercial manufacturers. Capitalizing on innovative materials such as Aerogel, Liquid Ceramic, and Kevlar, companies such as Corpo Nove in Italy and Engarde in the Netherlands are creating jackets, coats, and vests with unprecedented insulating properties that afford nomads and travelers from all walks of life the freedom and security to roam where they will.

High-tech garments are of particular value to women who have found themselves historically in positions of vulnerability. As artist Alicia Framis aptly notes, "safety comes from the feeling you are the owner of your own body and mind." Her *anti_dog* collection of street and formal wear promotes well-being through garments made of Twaron, a material that resists fire, bullets, and dog bites.

Product designers Adam Whiton and Yolita Nugent of No Contact challenge "existing power landscapes between men and women" through fashion that equalizes physical and social boundaries between the sexes. Their *No-Contact Jacket* is designed to return a sense of control to women in volatile situations by enabling them to electrically shock and block any would-be intruders.

Other garments are wired for personal pleasure such as the *JoyDress* by fashion designer Alexandra Fede. Integrated into its fabric are thin, flexible "vibra pads" which can be brought into motion at the touch of a button on a user-controlled command pad. The dress enhances body consciousness and can be used in playful ways according to the program selected by its wearer. As with all of the garments in this chapter, Fede's creations are non-aggressive means of extending one's physical and social boundaries.

In some instances, apparel in this chapter borders on architecture. Outfits such as Stefan Wischnewski's *warm up suit* and Jurgen Bey's *S.L.A.K.* suits resemble everyday sportswear but expand, fold out, or inflate to accommodate more than one person. Likewise, the individual pieces in artist Martina Salzberger's *24hr kit* can be unrolled and built onto each other to form conventional skirts, tops, and bottoms but also totes, provisional blankets, and screens.

Whether high– or low-tech, professionally manufactured or handmade, all of the garments in this chapter take over where our bodies leave off, and prove that utility wear need not be limited to drab working-class uniforms or aggressive and scary riot gear.

Hoodlum welding Hoods

The bog-standard welding mask is a drab piece of kit. There was a time when visiting a workshop meant being confronted by a team of identical-looking workers all decked out in the same navy-blue overalls and the same dreary black welding hoods. Hoodlum welding is doing its best to add some character to that uniform scenario with its distinctive array of cartoon-style masks.

In the mid-1990s a pair of tattooed welders from Long Beach, California, hit upon the idea of manufacturing hoods in radically different styles. Since then, designs with names such as Burning Skull, Bulldog, Android, and Gorilla, have provided a much needed alternative to the basic black hood that was once the only option. Fresh styles are periodically introduced to keep the line vibrant and a recent introduction includes the Hollywood Hog complete with its own nose-ring and wraparound shades. Often it is through close

consultation with the firm's loyal customer base that new production models are determined and designed. Up-to-date innovations such as solar-powered self-darkening lenses can also be fitted to ensure the hoods perform successfully in the field.

Hoodlum's hoods were inspired by a long-standing tradition among members of the welding profession who customize their standard-issue headgear with striking paint-jobs and graffiti-style tags, much like skaters and surfers did with their boards. Welders aren't prescribed a uniform to conform to the given image of an institution but, like many other workers, they have to wear a mask as a safety precaution. Hoodlum recognizes that any uniform can strip its wearer of his or her own identity. Its comical range of helmets brings a bit of character into the workplace and maybe even gives its fans an added sense of pride when they're firing up their torches.

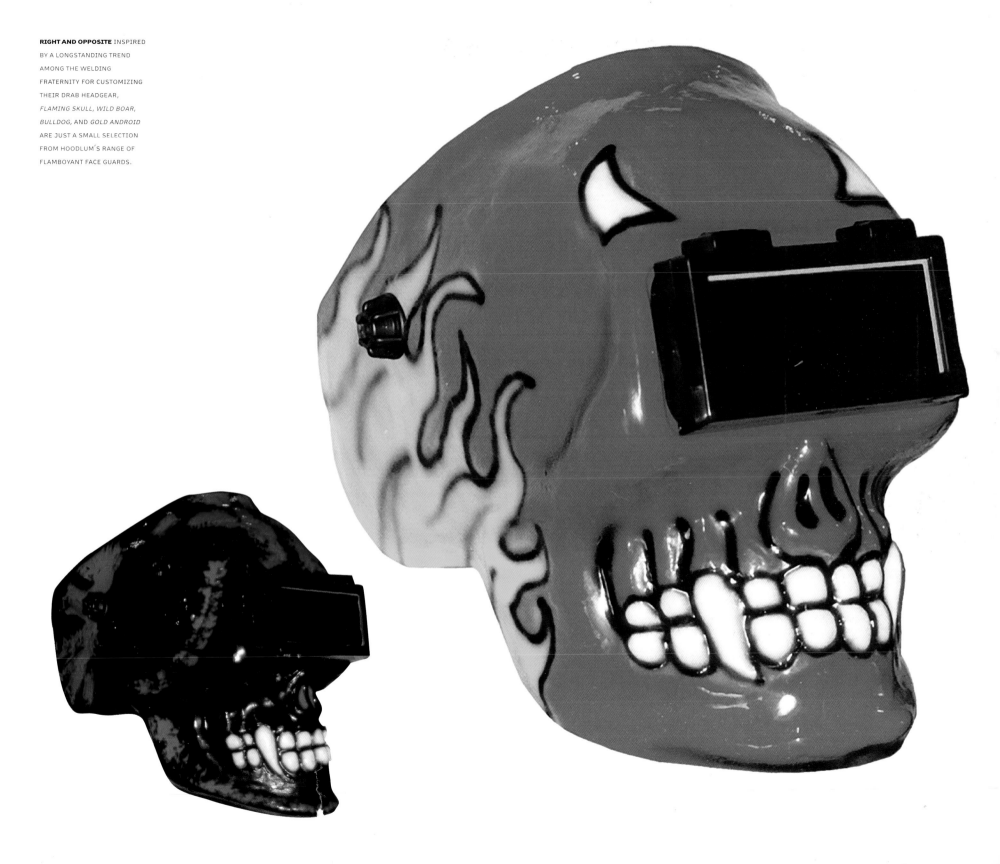

ALEXANDRA FEDE, ITALY

Antiviolence®, 2002
stressless™, 2002
joydress™, 2001

Alexandra Fede is a fashion designer and research scientist who wants clothing to take a more proactive role in everyday life. The designer equips garments such as those in her *Antiviolence* and *stressless* collections with extreme levels of protection, yet styles the clothes to look no different from any others that might be found hanging on the rails of saks, selfridges, or other up-market department stores. Fede's high-tech outfits have no trace of the techno-warrior about them. Instead, she chooses to hide the added features of her clothing behind natural-looking forms and materials.

Fede's *joydress* is a normal-looking dress fitted with a pleasure-giving massage device. The dress, made with the innovative material Lycra T400, has integrated into its fabric a series of thin, flexible "vibrapads" that can be programmed to vibrate and stimulate specific areas of the body. Fede conceived the dress as a playful piece of clothing used to stimulate the body's most sensitive areas and make the person wearing it feel aroused. The gentle massaging action encourages blood circulation and can revitalize the body like a dip in a Jacuzzi.

Antiviolence is a markedly different proposition. The collection of prototype garments is produced from a fabric that feels as light and soft as cashmere but is much tougher than steel. A dress made using the *Antiviolence* fabric offers protection from an array of potentially lethal hazards including gunshots, knife attacks, and even grenade blasts. The material has a special molecular compound that removes the force of any sudden impact by distributing it in a circular pattern across the fibers in its own structure.

Antiviolence clothing is non-flammable and offers high chemical and thermal resistance while also allowing maximum freedom of movement. The *Antiviolence* evening dress may give the appearance that a woman wearing one is dressed up for a smart reception when in fact she's fully equipped to take on a hail of bullets.

Likewise, garments in Fede's *stressless* collection may look nothing out of the ordinary, but they're able to shield the body from electromagnetic radiation. The clothes are made using a carbon fabric based on natural fibers that dissipates electrostatic charges and repels radioactive waves. Garments in both the *Antiviolence* and *stressless* collections are styled to look like everyday attire, a look that belies their status as 21st-century body armor.

OPPOSITE LEFT AND TOP LEFT
WOVEN INTO THE CORE
OF THE NATURAL THREADS
USED IN THE MANUFACTURE
OF THESE STRESSLESS™
GARMENTS IS A PROTECTIVE
CARBON FIBER THAT DISSIPATES
ELECTROSTATIC CHARGES WHILE
ALSO OFFERING A SHIELD
AGAINST ELECTROMAGNETIC
RADIATION.

OPPOSITE RIGHT HIDDEN IN
THE FABRIC OF FEDE'S
JOYDRESS™ ARE A NETWORK
OF SLIM, VIBRATING PADS THAT
CAN BE PROGRAMMED TO
MASSAGE DIFFERENT AREAS
OF THE BODY.

BELOW LEFT AND LEFT THE
SHARP EVENING DRESS IS PART
OF FEDE'S ANTIVIOLENCE®
COLLECTION. THE FABRIC
USED IS ABLE TO WITHSTAND
BULLETS, GRENADE BLASTS,
KNIFE ATTACKS, AND OTHER
FORMS OF EXTREME VIOLENCE.
SUCH LEVELS OF PROTECTION
ARE NEEDED TO SAFEGUARD
THE TECHNOGOLD DRESS, ONE
OF FEDE'S MOST ELABORATE
CREATIONS. THE DRESS IS MADE
FROM A SPECIALLY PRODUCED
GOLD DEVELOPED BY THE
MITSUBISHI MATERIALS
CORPORATION AND WEIGHS
OVER 30 KILOS.

HAL-3 (Hybrid Assistive Limb), 2004

RIGHT AND OPPOSITE THE ROBOTIC LOWER-BODY SUIT CONSISTS OF A FRAMEWORK TO SUPPORT THE USERS' LEGS, MOTORS AT THE KNEE AND HIP JOINTS THAT ASSIST MOVEMENT, TWIN BATTERY PACKS STRAPPED TO THE HIPS, SENSORS IN THE HEELS AND AROUND THE THIGHS, AND A BACK PACK THAT HOUSES THE COMPUTERIZED CONTROL SYSTEM FOR THE WHOLE ENSEMBLE.

Movies such as *Robocop* depict nightmarish visions of a future where men merge with machines to become invincible, out-of-control killers. Professor Yoshiyuki Sankai has a very different vision. He sees robotic body suits coming to the aid of people with physical disabilities or weakened limbs.

HAL-3 is a lower-body robotic suit designed to help those who have difficulty walking. The outfit consists of a backpack, which powers, monitors, and drives the whole system, and a mechanized supporting frame worn around the hips, legs, and feet. Built-in sensors detect when the user wants to move by picking up the faint electrical signals transmitted from the brain to the muscles in the lower body. An on-board computer analyzes the signals and deciphers exactly what the user wants to do. Motors positioned at the hips and knees start-up instantly to assist the movement. Timing is all-important. If the motors were to kick-in a fraction of a second too late then the suit would be more hindrance than help.

Sankai has been developing the prototype *HAL-3* since 1998 at the Cybernics Laboratory of the University of Tsukuba, Japan, and is marketing a production model through his company Cyberdyne Inc. The prototype suit weighs 15–17 kg depending on the set-up, but it does not feel so heavy because the heel section takes the weight. The commercial version is made with lighter, smaller components and weighs considerably less

at 10 kg. Each *HAL-3* unit is customized to the specific needs and physical conditions of the person it is intended for. An adaptable version is also available to organizations such as hospitals that need it to be available to a variety of people.

The professor first initiated the idea of a robotic suit in 1995 and has long been passionate about finding ways of supplementing human functions with machines. As a child he was fascinated by the robots portrayed in comics such as *Cyborg 009* and the novel *I, Robot*. They gave him an interest in using robotic devices to help people expand their physical abilities. With *HAL-3* he has brought those ideas to life and expanded enormously the functions a pair of pants might perform in the future. The prototype *HAL-3* might not look very much like a piece of clothing but Sankai is aiming to make the suit light enough to be worn like a regular garment.

STEFAN WISCHNEWSKI, GERMANY/SWEDEN

The Fortune on My second skin, size: L, 2003
warm up, 2002
wind Bag, size: XL, 2004
work Place, 2001

munich-based artist stefan wischnewski has been exploring the structural possibilities of industrial and lightweight fabrics to join objects and people for many years. whether through collaborations with seamstresses who make alterations for him or through pieces he sews himself, wischnewski's artworks cross the borders of art, design, fashion, and architecture and open up new ways of thinking about how the fields might interact.

"All of my wearable pieces consist of small and mid-sized transformations that bestow upon an object, and often a person, another specially focused meaning," says wischnewski. In *The Fortune on My second skin,* for example, wischnewski applied an old-school tattoo—slightly altered to include the name of his girlfriend "sarah"—onto a well-worn, blue-jean jacket. By enlarging the jacket's shoulder and arm, it was possible to stitch on the tattoo while wearing the jacket. The resulting deformed shoulder acts as a surrogate for wischnewski's real skin and bears testament to the ridiculous surgical procedure enacted upon it in the name of fashion.

warm up is another reworking of a popular casual-wear staple. In this case, wischnewski slightly altered two tracksuits and recombined them into a slip-cover of sorts that, when stretched over an exercise bike and its rider, morphs the two opposites into a new unit — a symbiosis of man and machine. The "combi suit," as he refers to it, locks the unlikely pair in an intimate hug and makes it difficult for

one to break free of or be distinguished from the other. when not in use and hung on a clothing stand, the suit looks like two lovers holding hands and assumes a surreal, anthropormorphic quality.

wischnewski is originally from a small town near Kiel, a seafaring community on the northern coast of Germany whose imagery and symbols crop up in *wind Bag,* a garment for beach visitors. The one-sided contraption is made of plastic sheeting—of the sort used for wind blocks or beach accessories—and straps onto the wearer's body at key connection points: the head, shoulder, arm, waist, and leg. The title of the piece comes from a North German yeast pastry which plumps up when baked, although wischnewski's version doesn't require heat to expand. Rather, a strong gust of wind serves to unroll its triangular shape from the body. when fully extended, it resembles a half-built tent and flutters like a bird's wing. The triangle is a typical symbol associated with shipping traffic along the coastline and here is used as a means of extension and signing. As in all of wischnewski's creations, a transformation of the body occurs through the relationship of material to person and place.

LEFT *WARM UP* JOINS HUMANS AND THEIR EXERCISE MACHINES WITHIN A COMBI SUIT BUILT FOR TWO.

LEFT FOR *THE FORTUNE ON MY SECOND SKIN,* WISCHNEWSKI ENLARGED THE SHOULDER AND ARM OF A BLUE JEAN JACKET SO THAT HE COULD APPLY A TATTOO ONTO IT AS THOUGH ETCHING IT DIRECTLY INTO HIS "SKIN."

TOP THE JACKET UNDER CONSTRUCTION.

ABOVE THE ARTIST DISPLAYS THE FINISHED PRODUCT.

stefan wischnewski, germany/sweden

OPPOSITE *WIND BAG* IS A TEMPORARY EXTENSION FOR ONE SIDE OF THE BODY THAT FLUTTERS LIKE A BIRD'S WING OR FLAG WHEN CAUGHT BY A GUST OF WIND.

LEFT *WORK PLACE* REFERS TO THE BLUE COVERALLS WORN BY HANDWORKERS IN GERMANY. AS ALTERED BY ARTIST STEFAN WISCHNEWSKI, THE 100 PERCENT COTTON UNIFORM BECOMES A FIXED OBJECT, WITH A BASE DETERMINED BY THE RADIUS OF AN ARM, AND HELD DOWN WITH RED-AND-WHITE SECURITY TAPE OF THE TYPE FOUND IN THE INDUSTRIAL WORKPLACE. AS IN OTHER WORKS BY WISCHNEWSKI, *WORK PLACE* EXPLORES THE STRUCTURAL AND EXPRESSIVE LIMITS OF CLOTHING, HERE BECOMING A METAPHOR FOR A WORKER IN HIS COSTUME, IN HIS TASK, AND IN HIS SPACE.

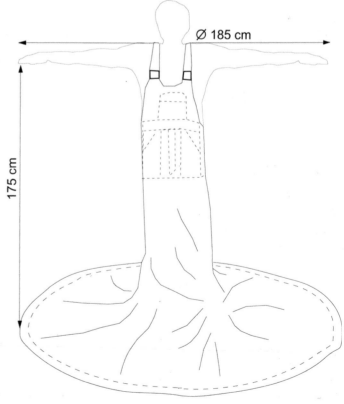

Ø 185 cm

175 cm

anti_dog, 2000 & ongoing

...allowed to be...

...oking at your face makes me sick ©

...ve don't want a foreigner for this job ©

since its launch at Paris Fashion Week in 2000, *Anti_Dog* has continued to grow into an extraordinary collection of over twenty provocative garments. Spanish artist Alicia Framis initiated the project while she was living in Berlin. The artist was warned about a district of the city that is notorious for its gangs of racist skinheads who use vicious dogs to attack immigrants and other people they take a dislike to. Framis was told that, as a woman with dark skin, it would not be safe for her to walk alone in that district. So the artist developed a collection of clothing that would offer protection against the dog bites and other forms of abuse.

The clothes in the *Anti_Dog* collection are made from Twaron, an ultra-strong fabric that is used in the manufacture of bullet-proof and stab-proof vests. Framis worked in collaboration with several well-known fashion designers to realize the outfits, which are styled after the iconic fashions of André Courrèges, Coco Chanel, Hussein Chalayan, and Christian Dior, among others. The classic styling and the golden fabric give the clothes an added luxurious appeal. They are very elegant, but also very tough.

After the presentation of the first series of outfits Framis began making garments with the same tough material in collaboration with groups of women at community workshops held in several European cities. In Helsingborg, Sweden, the artist worked with a group who were campaigning for improvements to the street lighting in areas of the city where they felt unsafe. Together they created a series of outfits that are illuminated and therefore bring light into the dark streets and alleyways that are the source of so much fear.

Framis also undertook a residency in Birmingham in the UK and worked with a group of local women to produce a collection of enormous gowns that were used to occupy the city's main square. The garments are adorned with bold phrases such as "This is not your country" and "I don't want a foreigner for this job"—quotes relating the personal experiences, fears, and hopes of the women who took part in the workshops. These quotes are also copyrighted in a challenge to the ownership of such phrases. Fashion is a powerful weapon for Framis. She uses it in a seductive and compelling way to address issues such as verbal and physical abuse, racism, and violence against women.

Alicia Framis, spain

Absolute zero, 1999
oricalco, 2001

ABOVE AND TOP RIGHT

ABSOLUTE ZERO, 1999.
AEROGEL, FABRIC, PET.
DESIGNED BY MAURO TALIANI
FOR CORPO NOVE, ITALY.
AEROGEL SUPPLIED BY
MARKETECH INTERNATIONAL,
PORT TOWNSEND,
WASHINGTON. AEROGEL IS ONE
OF THE LIGHTEST SUBSTANCES
ON EARTH AND IS AN EXCELLENT
INSULATOR. HERE PACKS OF
POWDERED AEROGEL HAVE
BEEN TUCKED BETWEEN LAYERS
OF A JACKET FOR ULTIMATE
PROTECTION.

BELOW LEFT AND OPPOSITE

ORICALCO, 2001. FABRIC MADE
FROM 50 PERCENT TITANIUM
AND A MIX OF OTHER ALLOYS.
DESIGNED BY MAURO TALIANI
FOR CORPO NOVE, BACAGLI,
AND TEXTEAM, ITALY. WHEN
COOL, THE SHIRT CAN
"REMEMBER" SHAPES
EMBEDDED INTO IT. WHEN
EXPOSED TO A BLAST OF HOT
AIR, THE WRINKLES ARE
"FORGOTTEN."

corpo nove is the brand name of the manufacturing firm karada italia srl. karada was started in 1996 by ex-journalist Federico Pagliai with the objective of injecting new viewpoints and ways of operating into the world of fashion. comprised of a diverse group of individuals with experience in different areas of fashion, karada has strived to maintain an "open-mindedness and ability to adapt to all sorts of projects." since its founding, this goal has translated into research and communication with partners as diverse and unlikely as NASA and ESA (European Space Agency) and Italian, American, and Australian universities.

The firm is unique in its integrative approach to fashion. It's not just a label for the garments it produces but a new method of producing clothing *per se.* The company is made up of two interconnected and collaborative halves and functions more like a laboratory than a traditional couture house. There is the research side, called Grado Zero Espace, whose task it is to discover and experiment with new materials and their potential applications. Then there is the creative side, corpo nove, headed by designer Mauro Taliani, that produces garments. This R&D approach ensures the transfer of technology to fashion in meaningful and considered ways that combine continuity with change, tradition with innovation. Above all, the firm is concerned with quality of life and meticulously designed garments, so much so that it often shares its findings and makes its expertise available to other companies.

one of the first garments produced by corpo nove—and one its first collaborations with NASA—was the *Absolute zero* jacket made of Aerogel. This smoky-blue, silicon-based solid has a porous sponge-like structure and is one of the lightest substances on earth, 1,000 times less dense than glass. The substance was invented in the 1930s and is an excellent insulator. In 1999, for example, it was used to insulate the Mars Pathfinder. Because of Aerogel's beneficial applications for extreme weather or atmospheric conditions, such as the Arctic Circle or outer space, corpo nove sewed bags of powdered Aerogel between two layers of fabric to create an incredibly warm and ingeniously lightweight outdoor coat.

corpo nove's *oricalco* men's shirt is equally smart—both in technology and form. At first glance, it resembles a fancy evening shirt fit for the club circuit. But its shimmery, silky appearance belies the strength and durability of the titanium woven into the shirt's fabric. The titanium allows the garment to alter its appearance depending on what the temperature is. In cool-to-room temperatures, the shirt will hold and "remember" wrinkles or any other 3-D forms which are embedded into its structure. when the temperature heats up, creases and wrinkles relax and may be flattened out. This means the shirt can be "ironed" while on the body, if desired, by exposing it to a blast of hot air, such as from a hair dryer.

unlike other fashion labels that churn out seasonal collections which claim to reflect the contemporary, karada "invents" clothes that are truly in sync with today because they derive from research into societal conditions beyond the realm of fashion.

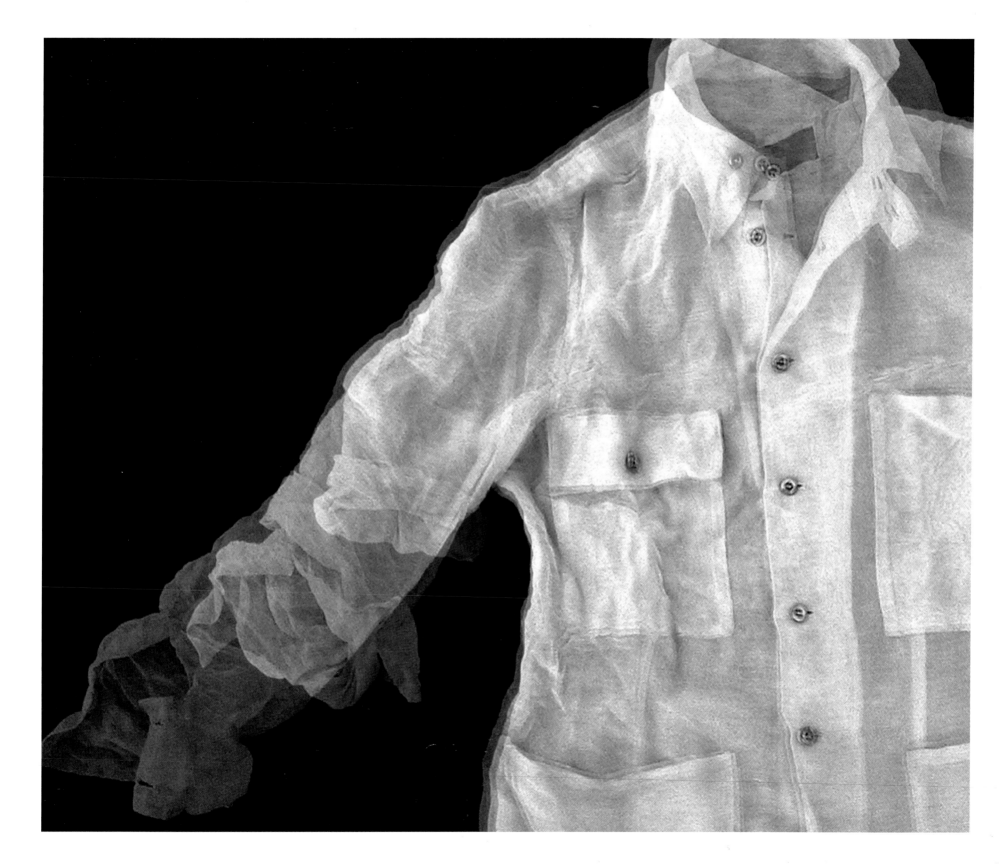

RIGHT AND OPPOSITE

RESEMBLING HUNTING AND
FORMAL ATTIRE, THE CIVILIAN
BODY ARMOR BY ENGARDE IS
DESIGNED TO BLEND IN WHILE
ALSO PROVIDING MAXIMUM
PROTECTION FOR THE UPPER
BODY. THE INDIVIDUAL VESTS
ARE MADE FROM ADVANCED
BULLETPROOF MATERIALS SUCH
AS DYNEEMA®, KEVLAR®, AND
TWARON WITH AN OUTER LAYER
COMPRISED OF COOLMAX, AND
COME IN A VARIETY OF STYLES,
COLORS, AND PATTERNS.

The catalogue images of the latest body armor from Dutch manufacturer ENGarde look more like advertisements for sta-pressed shirts than flak jackets. Yet behind the armor's flawless, smooth shells lies an internal network of high-tech materials that can stop a bullet, deter an ice pick, or ward off a knife attack.

Engineered for a broad range of uses, ENGarde's vests and jackets are made of Kevlar® and ceramic and polyethylene materials such as Dyneema®, Stabond®, Famostone, and Aristone. When combined, these materials lend the garments high-tensile strength, elasticity and buoyancy, as well as heat resistance. Exterior fiber shells increase comfort and range of motion and make the armor waterproof, windproof, and breathable.

Once the fashion staple of cops and soldiers, body armor is becoming commonplace in civilian circles. The fear factor certainly figures large in the supply and demand. In today's atmosphere of terrorist threats, heightened by the media's portrayal of urban streets as war zones and airports as potential death traps, survival clothing has crossed over into the mainstream to actually become "fashionable." A list of suggested clients on the ENGarde website includes people one wouldn't normally imagine in riot gear: coast guards, taxi drivers, public transportation employees, business-men, bureaucrats, foreign honored guests, VIPs, entertainers, sports players, public stars, watch officers for the mentally ill, calamity workers at industrial sites, "and everybody who wants to walk around feeling safe!"

It is not surprising, then, that the protective armor is marketed as if it were the latest fashion, with different collections and models to choose from and a range of options, colors, patterns, and prices. The "civilian" line, for example, features smart, bodice-hugging, black-and-white vests that might actually be mistaken for part of a three-piece suit. The dapper gentlemen wearing these "Eagle Eye" models are portrayed as sexy James Bond-type action figures, well-heeled businessmen, or bespectacled intellectuals. At the other end of the spectrum are more sporty jackets in autumn colors or camouflage patterns that depict their wearers in leisure mode.

That the garments are easy to wear and easy on the pocketbook—a civilian model ranges from 460 to 710 euros—make ENGarde body armor the perfect example of clothes that literally work for you, providing "a secure protection of your life" the moment you put them on.

3-112 MARTINA SALZBERGER, GERMANY

working clothes, 1999
Hats, 1998
24-Hour-Kit, 2000

RIGHT AND OPPOSITE
ENCASING THE BODY IN TIGHT
VINYL, MARTINA SALZBERGER'S
WORKING CLOTHES RESTRICT
MOVEMENT AND ARE INTENDED
TO SERVE AS METAPHORS FOR
SOCIETAL LIMITATIONS.

FOLLOWING PAGES, LEFT
CLEANING LADIES AT MUNICH'S
ACADEMY OF FINE ART MODEL
SALZBERGER'S HATS.
SALZBERGER HELPED THE
WOMEN SELECT HATS THAT
MATCHED THEIR PERSONALITY.

FOLLOWING PAGES, RIGHT
FORM FOLLOWS FUNCTION IN
SALZBERGER'S *24-HOUR-KIT.*
COMPRISED OF ROLLED FABRIC
SQUARES THAT JOIN TOGETHER
WITH VELCRO STRIPS TO FORM
CLOTHING AND BAGS, THE FORM
EACH OUTFIT TAKES DEPENDS
ON THE NEEDS OF THE USER.

For artist Martina Salzberger, the borders between art and fashion are extremely fluid. Salzberger began her art career as a painter but changed her focus to object-making in a series of hats created during a residency in Brussels. Salzberger found great inspiration in the city's architecture and streetlife, and references to both may be found in her quirky head coverings. A bamboo-shaped top hat reinterprets a piece of music she heard in the subway, while a prickly beret echoes the landscape of the city's French-style rooftops. An open-side model that resembles a bicycle helmet and is made of artificial hair was inspired by the coiffeurs of Brussels's African population, whom Salzberg encountered for the first time. More like wearable sculptures than head protection, Salzberger's hats push the structural and conceptual possibilities of traditional millinery.

A project called *working clothes* represents Salzberg's second foray into textiles. Resembling straightjackets, the tight-fitting garments were designed to reflect what Salzberger sees as the irony of the contemporary artistic condition. "Even though artists are self-employed and historically considered free agents, they are just as tied up in their choices as anyone else, sometimes so much so that they reach a position where it is difficult, if not impossible, to do their work,"

says Salzberger. Echoing her assertion, the vinyl jackets, skirts, and leg coverings exert a structural force on the body's limbs and bind and restrict their wearer into fetal-like positions of submission.

Salzberger's *24-Hour-Kit,* on the other hand, goes in a completely different direction to offer a wider range of movement through a greater choice of garments. The kit consists of a velcro harness that is strapped onto the upper body. This structure holds up to eight vertical cloth packets that when unrolled may be joined together to form pants, tops, skirts, jackets, and totes. Each unit is reversible, with one side being made of water-resistant fabric and the other side of a breathable mesh that doubles as pockets. Because it is a modular system, the combinations are endless. How and when the pieces are used is dependent on the situation and needs of the wearer. For urbanites, frequent travelers, or anyone on the go, the *24-Hour-Kit* is a highly flexible clothing system that doubles as its own light luggage.

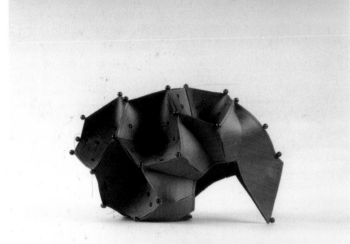

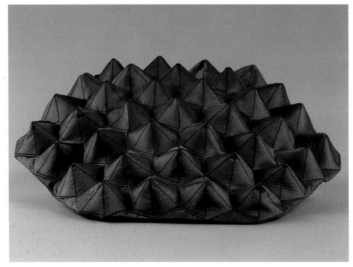

martina salzberger, germany

S.L.A.K. (for the Auping Foundation), 2001

ABOVE AND RIGHT THE THREE GARMENTS IN THE *S.L.A.K.* VARY IN APPEARANCE BUT, JUST LIKE SNAILS, THEY ALL CARRY SHELTERS ON THEIR BACKS.

Dutch designer Jurgen Bey is well known for his unconventional product designs. *S.L.A.K.* sees the designer switch his attention to both fashion design and architecture in a series of three garments that expand to form air-filled houses.

"slak" is the Dutch word for a snail and Bey's design was inspired in part by this humble creature. Just as a snail carries its house around on its back, Bey's *S.L.A.K.* collection consists of three jackets that enable people to do the same. Fastened to the back of each jacket is a voluminous piece of material resembling an oversized pocket, which can be inflated to form a relatively large shelter. No complicated gadgets or troublesome switches are needed to perform the operation. The featherweight material needs only a slight breeze to keep it inflated. In fact, the material is so light that it has no need for any structural support other than air.

Ken, Karl, and Kimberley are the first three members of the Suits Light Architecture family. Ken is a metallic bomber jacket, which carries a spherical balloon resembling some of the earliest communications satellites. Karl is a cubic inflatable shelter hooked up to a yellow overcoat, and Kimberley is a garment that expands into an enormous blob-like form. Bey's garments/dwellings are very different from the highly functional pieces presented by Moreno Ferrari (see pages 32–35). The swollen, air-filled spaces born of Karl, Ken and Kimberley appear like cartoon thought-bubbles. They are delicate and dreamy and do not seem at all practical.

The simple garments and their equally simple shelters help bring architecture and fashion closer together. In an interview with Louise Schouwenberg in *Frame* magazine Bey asked, "why shouldn't objects have the ability to assume new roles whenever they feel the urge?" *S.L.A.K.* sees Bey take pieces of clothing and literally blow them up to architectural proportions while also transforming the identity of architecture with the fabric and the ephemeral nature of fashion. Most people tend to think of buildings as solid, permanent entities but Bey challenges that idea with his series of voluminous air-filled shelters that have plenty of bulk but very little weight.

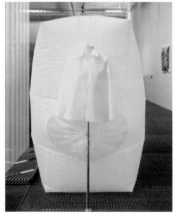

ABOVE AS THIS SEQUENCE OF
PHOTOGRAPHS ILLUSTRATE, ALL
IT TAKES IS A LIGHT BREEZE TO
SWELL THE *S.L.A.K.* WEARABLE
SHELTER TO MAMMOTH
PROPORTIONS.

no-contact jacket for women, 2003

RIGHT AND OPPOSITE IN ORDER TO DISCHARGE THE INCAPACITATING ELECTRIC SHOCK THE JACKET MUST FIRST BE ARMED AND THIS IS ACHIEVED BY ACTIVATING THE KEY-OPERATED SWITCH. ONCE THE JACKET IS ACTIVATED THE CHARGE IS RELEASED BY PRESSING ONE OF THE HAND-HELD BUTTONS. THIS CHARGE IS CONCEALED WITHIN THE JACKET'S OUTER SHELL, BUT BRIGHT AND AUDIBLE ARCS OF ELECTRICITY APPEAR BETWEEN THE SEAMS ON THE UPPER RIGHT SHOULDER TO ACT AS A CLEAR WARNING TO ANY WOULD-BE ASSAILANTS THAT THIS IS NO ORDINARY JACKET.

corsets, high-heel shoes, and tight-fitting dresses are all examples of female attire that restrict and limit mobility. In doing so, such items can render women exposed and vulnerable to attack. Adam Whiton and Yolita Nugent, the design team behind *no-contact*, aim to redress the balance and are fusing fashion and technology to instill women with greater feelings of power and security.

no-contact is worn like any other jacket, but when the wearer feels unsafe or threatened she is able to arm an in-built defense mechanism that discharges a stinging electric shock. The wearer prepares the jacket by switching it on via a key-operated switch. once the system is armed, a flashing LED light acts as a warning to any would-be assailants that the current is ready to be discharged. If the assailant chooses to ignore the warning and tries to grab the woman, she can hit either one of two palm-held panic buttons to release the current around the jacket, which, on contact, strikes the attacker down with a debilitating high-voltage shock.

A woman wearing the *no-contact jacket* is shielded from the electrical current by a layer of insulating rubber that lines the whole garment. The sleeves are necessarily elongated to protect the hands from rogue electrical charge, and to provide cradles for the twin panic buttons. By positioning a panic button in the palm of each hand the designers are making use of one of the body's natural responses to fear, which is to clench the fists. Therefore, even if the woman under attack feels so afraid that she forgets what to do, her natural reactions will kick-start the shock. The designers are keen to stress that the *no-contact jacket* is "not a magic solution to any assault situation." *no-contact* is designed to be most useful in situations where the assailant uses physical force such as in

sexual assaults, as opposed to attacks involving a gun or knife. However, the jacket does raise some alarming concerns as to what might happen should a woman choose to use it as an offensive weapon rather than a means of defense. In response, the designers state that statistically speaking men commit a disproportionately larger amount of aggravated assaults and forcible rapes than women do. "We've gotten a huge response from women wanting to purchase the jackets," add the designers, "and we feel it is more alarming that women in our society deem this [type of clothing] necessary to wear on a daily basis." *no-contact* is just one illustration of how fashion design is responding to a desire among young women to be free to take risks, to be more mobile and active, and to step out and explore areas where they might have once felt threatened.

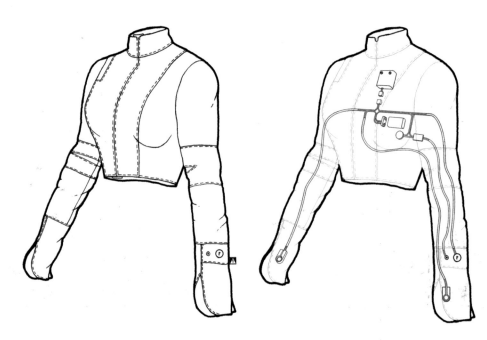

CHAPTER 4

DRESS CODE

"The management reserves the right to refuse admission. Smart dress only. No hoodies. No sneakers. No caps." Arbitrary dress codes aren't only for pretentious nightclubs where stern-faced security go about their business of separating the in from the out.

Everyday people are judged by what they choose to wear. Our clothes speak volumes and this chapter includes designers, artists, and others who use clothes to transmit messages. Different occasions call for different modes of dress. It wouldn't be proper to roll up at an exclusive country club wearing spandex shorts and a sequined muscle vest. Conforming to the dress code of a particular club or group shows a desire to belong, but what if that group doubts the authenticity of your appearance or questions your loyalty? This sense of not belonging is an important theme in the work of Chinese-Australian artist Greg Leong. From a distance his exquisite garments may appear to be the typical attire of a Chinese waitress or a costume from the Peking opera, but on closer inspection it becomes clear that these outfits aren't what they seem. The real story is revealed in the details. Leong explores his family's heritage in these uneasy outfits and draws attention to the rejection felt by those who are made to feel they don't belong. Similarly, the artist Rubén Ortiz Torres reworks the embroidered details on baseball caps to give them new and provocative meanings.

Lucy Orta, on the other hand, uses fashion to build a greater sense of belonging. Body suits, often created in community workshop events, are fitted with umbilical attachments to form physical bonds between the people who wear them. Participants in such events are connected by the very fabric of their dress and also by the uniform nature of the outfits. However, their individual identities are not quashed but flourish in the decoration they apply. Making connections and bringing people closer together are also strong influences on the *Tape* collection devised by Grit and Jerszy Seymour. The Berlin-based couple replaced the traditional needle and thread with swathes of adhesive tape to bind their bold outfits together.

Clothes can be used to transmit all kinds of messages. For young British designer, Victoria Berry, the message is that more women are keen on shooting birds. Berry has refashioned examples of traditional British shooting attire to make them more suitable for women who want to participate in the sport. American artist Cookie Gluck makes bizarre costumes shaped like medical instruments and body parts. These are used as flamboyant promotional tools at trade fairs and sales conventions for the pharmaceuticals' industry. These outfits can be seen as elaborate versions of the classic, slogan-festooned T-shirt. It doesn't matter on which side of the fence you are sitting; you can always find a T-shirt to proudly express your opinion. A T-shirt put out by Alternative Tentacles, the record label established by former Dead Kennedys vocalist Jello Biaffra, featured a red silhouette of a prisoner behind an enlarged bar code. The strap line beneath it read: "Just wait till these are tattooed on your wrist." It was a stark warning that if we weren't vigilant we would become prisoners of technology. The bars that keep us confined needn't be made of steel, but a code carrying detailed personal information tattooed on to our skin or even a pattern on a piece of clothing.

A much more positive view of the potential offered by the fusion of clothing and new technology is presented by the London based designers christopher J. Glaister and Michelle shakallis, and california-based artist Anne Niemetz. Glaister and shakallis have developed a series of knitted garments decorated with barcode-style stripes. A simple tune is translated into a barcode to create the pattern and when scanned by a modified cell phone, the coded tune can be used as a musical ring tone. The designers are keen to develop new ways of interacting with computers, which is also true of Anne Niemetz. Digital technology is commonplace in the music business but computers can occasionally be limiting when it comes to performing on stage. Niemetz's *stretching LA* project is just one of the artist's investigations into wearable musical instruments. Four performers stretch their suspenders to play back samples of talk show host Larry King.

stretching LA and the *CODE Ring Tone* garments sit in stark contrast to the work of Japanese fashion designer Kei Kagami. The former architect creates garments with pieces of old machinery to illustrate the beauty he sees in the industrial era. Kagami produced the collection out of sheer frustration with contemporary society's reliance on computer and microchip technology. His work is nostalgic for the days when machines were easy to understand and when things went wrong they were easy to put right.

A makeover extravaganza for a chinese–australian karaoke queen, 2003

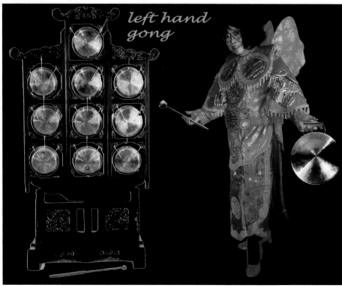

The "waitress uniform at the Ding Kam chinese Aussie Meat Pie Palace" may look like the typical uniform of a chinese waitress, but on closer inspection it becomes clear that this waitress works in no ordinary chinese restaurant. The chef has rejected the usual stir-fry and noodle dinners in favor of Australia's "fair dinkum" dish, the meat pie.

The costume is part of series of four works presented collectively under the title "A Makeover Extravaganza for a chinese–australian Karaoke Queen." The collection, aimed at a chinese–australian in search of a cultural makeover, consists of two suitcases worth of makeover gear: two costumes that appear to the uninitiated typically chinese and two that represent the most heroic examples of Australian men's work wear, the Drizabone coat and the flannelette shirt. However, none of these costumes are what they first appear to be. Their stories only become clear on closer inspection of the details.

Leong uses decorative embroidered patterns to question the very origins of the Australian phrase "fair dinkum," meaning genuine or authentic. Legend has it that this most Australian of phrases was actually made popular by chinese gold prospectors hoping to make their fortune in the Australian Gold Rush of the 19th century. "Ding kam," meaning

real or top gold, were apparently the words they shouted on discovery of the prized yellow ore.

The "opera Frock for a Giant chinese–australian warrior Diva" is a monstrous theatrical costume created out of a collision between chinese opera and Australian country music. The "True Blue" side of the costume is decorated with Australian country greats, while the "Pure Gold" side features stars of the Peking and cantonese opera; one of the Australians, however, has slipped on to the chinese side. In "Flannelette Carmen" and the accompanying piece, "Queen-sized Quilt for a cold Night out with Real Men," Leong undermines the manliness of the Australian flannelette work shirt by decorating a series of them with ladylike black lace. The clearly legible labels point to the origins of the shirts, which were apparently "Made in China."

Leong uses costume to explore his own chinese–australian heritage while also challenging accepted notions of identity, masculinity, belonging, and authenticity. His outfits are an uneasy clash of Australian and chinese cultural symbols. They do their best to accommodate the two idealistic notions of authentic chineseness and authentic Australianness, yet none of them could ever be considered as anything but synthetic by either side.

BELOW "YELLOW ON THE OUTSIDE, BLACK ON THE INSIDE," THE SLOGAN OF LEONG'S *DING KAM CHINESE AUSSIE MEAT PIE PALACE*, IS A REFERENCE TO A MALICIOUS TERM USED AGAINST THE PEOPLE OF VIETNAM DURING THE WAR WITH THE USA.

GREG LEONG, china/australia

BELOW THE COUNTRY'N'WESTERN
YOKE FROM THE *WARRIOR DIVA*
COSTUME IS DECORATED WITH
STARS FROM THE PEKING AND
CANTONESE OPERA INCLUDING
YAM KIM FAI AND MEI LANGFANG,
WHO SIT ALONGSIDE LEGENDS
OF AUSTRALIAN COUNTRY MUSIC
SUCH AS SLIM DUSTY AND JEAN
STAFFORD.

Baseball Hats, 2004

RIGHT RUBÉN ORTIZ TORRES IS A DEVOTED BASEBALL FAN WHO COLLECTS CARDS, CAPS, AND OTHER MEMORABILIA. HE FIRST CONSIDERED BASEBALL AND ITS RELATED SOUVENIRS AS AN ARTISTIC MEDIUM TO BE EXPLORED AFTER ALTERING A "MALCOLM X" CAP HE HAD RECEIVED AS A GIFT FROM AN AFRICAN–AMERICAN FRIEND TO READ "MALCOLM MEX," REFLECTING HIS OWN HERITAGE. SINCE THEN HE HAS ALTERED CAPS FROM TEAMS SUCH AS THE CLEVELAND BROWNS AND THE SAN DIEGO PADRES.

OPPOSITE ALTERED CHICAGO BLACKHAWKS AND SAN DIEGO STATE UNIVERSITY AZTECS CAPS.

colors, logos, symbols, and even brand names are powerful transmitters of social messages and, depending on how they're combined and worn, send specific signals about an individual's affiliations and personal beliefs. The rise of sporting attire as acceptable everyday leisure wear has played an interesting role within the coded language of fashion. Basketball jerseys, football tricots, and baseball caps are no longer just for athletes and children. For teens and adults alike, baseball hats are a popular and widespread means of expressing everything from team spirit to political ideology. Their front brims function like mobile mini-billboards.

For multimedia artist Rubén Ortiz Torres, who was born in Mexico but has lived in Los Angeles since 1990, the baseball cap is a fertile area for cross-cultural experimentation. By playing with the aesthetics of various hats—that is, rearranging or altering the words, symbols, and decorations applied to them—he has produced a series of hybrid head coverings that play off the commercialization and kitschification of emblems and insignia, and result in the creation of new cultural meanings.

Ortiz Torres's reworkings range from the lighthearted to the ironic to the politically

charged. A Chicago Blackhawks cap is taken back to its "roots" through Torres's application of Native American beadwork and a feather. For a San Diego Padres cap, he intertwined sports and religion by adorning the hat with Hispanic milagros, an image of Juan Soldado (the patron saint of the border and migrants), and small votive portraits. In a poignant and humorous tribute to the Jewish baseball legend Sandy Koufax, Ortiz Torres embroidered the logo of the L.A. Dodgers onto a traditional yarmulke. More far-reaching social critique may be found on an L.A. Kings hockey cap. By simply inserting the name "Rodney" above the word "King," Ortiz Torres refocused the message towards Rodney King, the African–American victim of police brutality in Los Angeles in 1991. Likewise, a Malcolm X cap is recoded into "Malcolm Mex" and "Mexico" by the addition of new letters.

Earlier this year, several of the hand-altered caps went on view at the Glassell School of Art in Houston, Texas. "Most Americans, even those who are not diehard baseball fans, are familiar with the images and objects associated with the game," noted Valerie Loupe, curator of the exhibition. "Ortiz Torres uses those images and objects to entice us to look at the game and

society in a different way."

For Ortiz Torres, the hats are meaningful new takes on the complex mix that is contemporary culture: "I alter baseball caps and their logos in order to recodify and recontextualize society's signs and ultimately to comment on the relation between aesthetics, history, mass media, culture, fashion, politics, and different communities divided by arbitrary rules and signs like sports teams."

RIGHT SELF-MADE L.A. DODGERS YARMULKE WITH "LA" EMBROIDERED AT THE CENTER AND A DECORATIVE BORDER.

FAR RIGHT L.A. KINGS BASEBALL CAP ALTERED TO REFER TO AFRICAN-AMERICAN RODNEY KING WHO CAME TO PUBLIC ATTENTION AFTER BEING MISHANDLED BY L.A. POLICE DURING A TRAFFIC STOP IN 1991.

Birds killing Birds, 2004

Disappointed by the lack of shooting attire available for women, fashion designer Victoria Berry decided to create her own range. Berry believes that the shooting outfits currently aimed at the female market are too expensive and not very practical. They are not, she claims, as hard wearing as those aimed at men, so female shoot enthusiasts often have to make do with wearing clothes cut for the male physique.

Shooting is a sport associated in the British Isles with the landed gentry. Indeed, it is often claimed that vast swathes of the British countryside have been preserved largely because of the long-standing affection for the sport. Although shooting is considered to be a male-dominated pursuit, Berry discovered that an increasing number of women are finding they have a passion for shotguns. Conditions on a shoot can be extremely harsh. Moorland in the British Isles is notoriously muddy, exposed, and rugged. The clothes that traditionally coped best with this environment are made with tough fabrics such as tweed in colors that offer camouflage against the heather-covered landscape. Berry's collection follows in this tradition but the designer has added a few wry ideas of her own.

The title of the collection is refreshingly un-PC. The English word "bird", as a cheeky term for a young woman, was effectively banned in the 1980s by the politically correct lobby who considered it to be patronizing and outdated. Berry wittily fuses this with the sport of shooting, which is also thought by some to be politically incorrect. While certain designers in recent years have created urban survival outfits that perpetuate anxiety and paranoia over inner-city gun crime, Berry has designed an exquisite range of clothes that positively encourages women to go out shooting.

Shotgun cartridges provide the basis for the motif used to decorate the *birds killing birds* blouse and field coat. "Some people", says Berry, "think they're lipsticks." The shooting theme also threads through into the details of the collection. The buttons on the jacket cuffs and the cuff links on the blouse are all made from the circular metal bases of shotgun cartridges. The collar, cuffs, and placket of the blouse are reinforced with tattersall checked cotton cloth, a favorite pattern of those interested in rural pursuits. The tweed jacket has a very feminine shape. The shoulders are wide and the waist tapers in before fanning out over the hips. The style is heavily influenced by Vivienne Westwood, a fashion designer renowned for her obsessive interest in traditional English dress.

The *birds killing birds* collection is both fashionable and practical. Berry wanted women to be able to look their best while out on the moors shooting grouse, but also be protected from the elements.

Tape, 2003

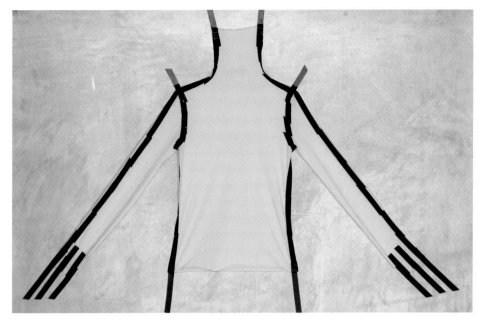

ABOVE, LEFT, AND FOLLOWING PAGES DESIGNED FOR THE "POST-INDUSTRIAL HERO" IN ALL OF US, THE T-SHIRTS, DRESSES, SKIRTS, PANTS, AND SWIMSUITS FOR MEN AND WOMEN BY GRIT AND JERSZY SEYMOUR ARE MADE OF STRETCH FABRICS HELD TOGETHER WITH BONDING TAPE. SUBVERTING THE TRADITIONAL RUNWAY PRESENTATION OF FASHION SHOWS, THE *TAPE* COLLECTIONS ARE PRESENTED AT ART VENUES AND GALLERIES. AT THE PALAIS DE TOKYO IN PARIS, FRANCE IN 2004, FOR EXAMPLE, (SEE P. 137) THE CLOTHES WERE HUNG FROM THE CEILING BY STRIPS OF THE SAME TAPE THAT HOLDS THEM TOGETHER. RATHER THAN SITTING LIFELESSLY ON A SHELF OR HANGER, THE CLOTHING SEEMED TO DANCE IN MID-AIR.

TAPE is not a material that *haute couture* houses might consider using to connect swatches of fabric. However, it is exactly the "thread" that Berlin design duo Grit and Jerszy Seymour envisioned as a way to literally and symbolically hold clothes together. The T-shirts, slacks, dresses, and swimwear in their year-old *Tape* collection are all made from sections of cotton jersey pasted together with a permanent, washable fabric tape. The sticky strips replace traditional seams and stretch with the clothing, providing an increased range of movement.

The *Tape* collection is the perfect example of what can happen when fashion comes into contact with industrial design and is, in fact, the result of a cross-disciplinary collaboration. Grit Seymour brings an informed understanding of the commercial fashion industry to the project. Born in former East Germany, she escaped to the west where she studied fashion at St. Martin's College of Art in London. She later worked for international fashion companies such as Donna Karan and Hugo Boss where she gained an insider's knowledge of how clothing is designed and produced. Jerszy Seymour was born in Berlin, grew up in London, and studied art at the Royal College. He is also a 3D artist and industrial designer whose work

has been widely exhibited.

By combining their separate pools of knowledge and individual strengths, the Seymours came up with a durable and flexible construction technique not typically associated with the production of clothing. Tape is generally used to mend paper or hang up messages, which is why the clothes have the direct and bold quality of posters or signage. Tape is also a widely available DIY staple and this association lends the garments a directness and personality usually seen in self-made clothes.

Because of the technique, each of the garments has a unique personality. Indeed, the clothes seem to want to tell us something. With their loud colors and crisscrossing, zigzagging, bisecting patterns, they conjure up all sorts of associations including maps, road signs, auto detailing, surgical stitches, and morse code.

Tape is more a statement than a new trend or style of clothing. "We felt that working with tape had a philosophical meaning that seemed very appropriate for our times," says Grit Seymour. According to the design duo, "It's like a Band-Aid; we're sticking things together and mending them."

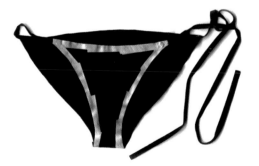

4-136

grit & jerszy seymour, germany

A key attraction of fashion for London-based designer Kei Kagami is that it allows him to express himself in a very direct way. Originally hailing from Tokyo, Kagami previously studied architecture and worked for a year as an assistant to the prominent Japanese architect Kenzo Tange. During this period, however, Kagami was also studying tailoring at night school and chose instead to pursue a career in fashion. "There isn't much of a boundary between architecture and fashion," says Kagami, "both deal with the space around the body." The designer enjoys the physical involvement he has with his work. "It's a medium to express myself with," he says, "I choose the material, cut the pattern, sew it together, and finally make it myself."

Kagami's passion for a hands-on approach to his work is sharply reflected in the spring/summer collection from 2004, which he named, *The Good Old Days—Industrial Revolution*. Computers were a major source of frustration for Kagami while he was putting the collection together. He wanted to design a series of garments that looked back to the industrial revolution, and illustrated the beauty of the mechanical devices associated with that era. "I have memories from my childhood of a time when life was not so much dominated by computers and microchips but with machines, which fulfilled simple and tangible actions." This nostalgia for a simpler age inspired the collection, which is shaped by a careful balance between mechanical devices and movements of the body.

Fine wool fabric is used to soften the impact of the machinery's hard image. The mechanical details are fully operational. They have a functional beauty and are not there solely for decorative purposes. Kagami's attraction to these mechanisms lies, in part, in the fact that they're relatively easy to understand. "With a machine you can see how it works. If it goes wrong you can often repair it by yourself," he explains, "I quoted industrial images to show just how great that era was."

kei kagami, japan

stretching L.A., 2003

RIGHT AND OPPOSITE THE FIRST EXHIBITION OF *STRETCHING L.A.* FEATURED A VIDEO OF THE FOUR PERFORMERS MAKING CONVERSATIONS WITH THE LARRY KING SAMPLES. A PAIR OF THE SUSPENDERS WAS ALSO ON DISPLAY FOR THE BENEFIT OF VISITORS TO SHOW THE VIDEO WASN'T JUST PUT TOGETHER IN AN EDIT SUITE. AS MUSICIANS GROW MORE AND MORE RELIANT ON COMPUTERS NIEMETZ'S WEARABLE MUSICAL INSTRUMENTS ALLOW PERFORMERS TO USE TECHNOLOGY IN A WAY THAT MAKES THE MOST OF PHYSICAL STAGE PRESENCE.

Anne Niemetz is a media artist with a passion for new ways of making music. For the piece *stretching L.A.* the artist invented a wearable instrument in the guise of a pair of suspenders that when stretched play snippets of talk-show host, Larry King.

The piece was made for the westweek 2003 LALALA exhibition at the Pacific Design center, Los Angeles. "I'd just moved to L.A. and was still suffering with culture shock," explains the artist, "I was watching a lot of Larry King's TV show and noticed how he always plays with his suspenders." Inspired by the chat show host Niemetz set out to create an alternative musical instrument by incorporating bend sensors into a pair of suspenders.

The bend sensors are hooked up to a sampler and play a different Larry King sound bite according to the amount of bend in the suspenders. Four performers took part in the *stretching L.A.* performance and each had access to four different samples. Any number of samples could be allocated to the suspenders but the more samples there are the more complicated the instrument is to play. The performers have to feel their way around the suspenders in order to find the right sounds, which can be scratched and replayed in the much the same way as a DJ can with records.

The result is very funny with the four performers jamming out and building conversations from the different samples with questions and responses ranging from, "Hi Los Angeles, what's life been like for you? – seems to get harsher all the time," to "Are you worried about the war? – yes." The way the performers physically interact with the instrument is an integral part of the show.

without moving their lips and using only suspender-stretching gestures the four Larry Kings raise questions about Los Angeles, its politics, and its people in a style that is amusing but also critical.

Niemetz has a strong interest in using interactive technology to make new sounds. In a piece similar to *stretching L.A.* the artist has an all-girl band perform using belts fitted with different sensors to make different sounds. "I like to mix up art, science, and popular culture," says the artist, "collaboration is my driving interest." As well as working with performers and musicians Niemetz also works closely with scientists and is very excited by the meeting of art and science. In such collaborations, says Niemetz, "the role of the artist is to make the scientists aware of just how important their discoveries are."

STRETCHING L.A.

▶ Anne Niemetz 2003

STRETCHING L.A.

▶ How are we today?

RIGHT *WHITE BLOODS CELLS* FOR AMGEN.

OPPOSITE *EYEBALL* FOR TAKEDA PHARMACEUTICALS.

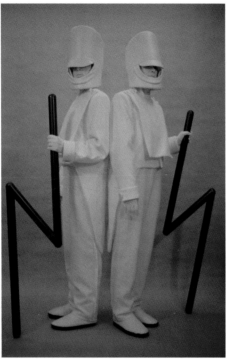

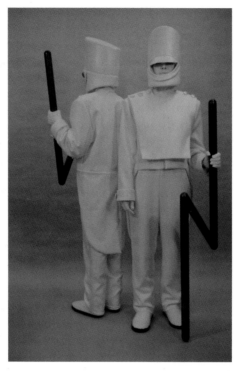

For more than twenty years, cookie gluck has been designing and fabricating mascots, prop objects, and wearable characters for numerous sports teams, businesses, films, and media events. "My work provides me with a varied media playground," gluck says. "In America, the media is very much the message. My work is not a product so much as a process of interacting with culture on its own terms."

Indeed, her costumes appeal to and reflect an American fascination with pop culture and products that promise the "good life." They are not so much disguises as caricatures of human traits in the form of loveable, huggable, saleable products. By increasing the scale of inanimate objects such as medical equipment, body parts, or pieces of food, gluck transforms them into funny and cute characters capable of leading independent lives and with personalities as unique as those of individual people. Hers is a perfect example of fashion that represents, promotes, advertises, and

above all transmits values and messages that may be easily read and interpreted by the public they are intended to reach. Like a business suit in a sales meeting, the costumes send signals through fashion.

Originally from Brooklyn, New York, gluck studied art at the university of wisconsin and later worked in theater. In 1970 she moved to chicago, Illinois, with the fledgling organic Theater Troupe and collaborated on the group's production of *WARP: A Science Fiction Epic Adventure in Serial Form*. Backstage she acquired hands-on experience with materials, methods, and production values. says gluck, "I found my visual voice backstage of productions, creating effects and making things look like something else." when the show moved to Broadway, gluck won the New York Drama Desk Award for its costumes.

By 1980 gluck's talent for producing spectacular effects and props was picked up on by commercial venues, enabling her to

found her own studio. In 1992 she moved her studio into a 2,500-square-foot facility where she continues to create new pieces and personally supervise the extensive operations. with the help of computer imaging, gluck is able to expand the range of her services from concept to product.

Gluck doesn't like to pigeon-hole what she does, preferring to let it exist in the overlap between many fields including art, fashion, design, and theater. "when I was in school I thought so much about what art was that it put a real crimp in my production," says gluck. "once I found myself actually working, I became a designer. what I actually design falls loosely in the area of wearable kinetic soft sculpture. Defining what I do is limiting."

RIGHT *TUMMY* FOR TAP PHARMACEUTICALS.

BELOW *MICROMETER* AND *IDS* AND *IDF DIGIMATIC INDICATORS* FOR MITUTOYO.

OPPOSITE *FOOT* AND *HEART* FOR TAKEDA PHARMACEUTICALS.

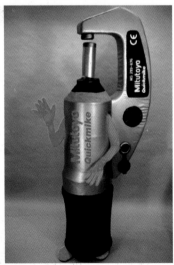
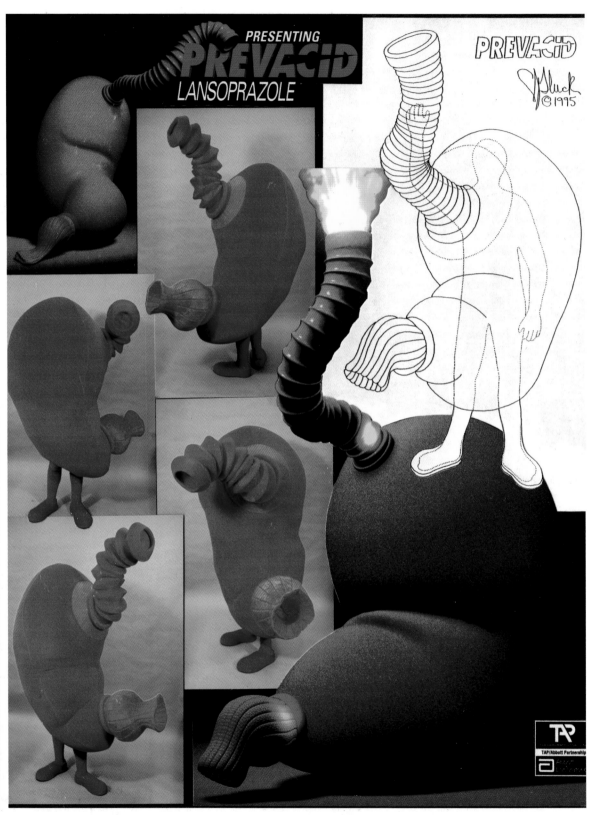

cookie gluck, USA

CODE Ring Tone Garments, 2004

CODE takes its inspiration from the trend for downloading personalized ring tones on to cell phones. The range of garments in the *CODE* series so far consists of two knitted scarves and a knitted sleeveless sweater. Each garment is decorated with a pattern made by translating a simple piece of music into a barcode. The coded pattern can be converted back into a tune by scanning it with a modified mobile camera/phone. The downloaded tune can then be used as the ring tone for that particular cell phone.

The project is the result of a collaborative effort between industrial designer Christopher J. Glaister and textile designer Michelle Shakallis. The pair developed the garments while they were studying at London's Royal College of Art for a competition sponsored by a major cell phone company. *CODE* is similar to Anne Niemetz's wearable technology project *stretching LA* (see pages 142–43) in that both parties are interested in developing overtly physical means for people to interact with computers. However, where Niemetz employs adjustable accessories hooked up to a sampler to generate music, Glaister and Shakallis have

translated sequences of musical notes into binary codes that form the basis of the decorative patterns on their garments. The patterns lend themselves particularly well to knitting, and create a rich contrast between the softness of the fabric and our traditional perception of technology as something that we experience through a shiny or hard interface, such as a screen or keyboard.

Ring tones are typically downloaded by visiting a website or by sending an SMS text message to a service provider. Glaister and Shakallis felt that this process was far too impersonal and so came up with the idea of using coded garments as a vehicle for sending information. "We want to put a tangible product into the hands of the consumer," says Glaister, who is interested in developing very physical ways for people to interact with technology. A customer will be able to walk into a store, buy a garment, and then scan it with their phone to download a new tune. It's a much more "hands-on" process than just prodding at a screen and gives an indication of how garments might be used to carry all sorts of information in the future.

Nexus Architecture intervention, Johannesburg Biennale, 1997
Transgressing Fashion #0204 (Nexus Architecture), sense and the city III, Victoria & Albert Museum, 2004

RIGHT FOR THE PIECE TITLED *TRANSGRESSING FASHION #0204* LUCY ORTA DRESSED FIFTY PARTICIPANTS IN MODIFIED COMBAT UNIFORMS AND CHOREOGRAPHED A MARCH AROUND FOUR GALLERIES AT THE VICTORIA AND ALBERT MUSEUM IN LONDON.

Lucy Orta mixes up fashion, architecture, and performance in influential works of art that encourage debate, explore new forms of communication, and build social bonds. The artist often employs combat uniforms and other military surplus paraphernalia as potent reminders of conflicts, displacement, and other appalling events.

For the piece titled *Transgressing Fashion #0204* Orta dressed fifty participants in modified combat uniforms boldly decorated with patterns and slogans in shimmering gold leaf. Reflective surfaces are a common motif in Orta's work. In this case they created a visual link between the uniforms and their grandiose surroundings. *Transgressing Fashion #0204* was created for the Victoria and Albert Museum in London. The participants moved in a choreographed parade around four of the museum's galleries wearing hoods like those worn by Iraqi prisoners of war or inmates at the notorious Camp X-ray detention center in Guantanamo Bay, Cuba.

The piece brings to mind modern-day conflicts but also reminds onlookers that the museum they are standing in is full of artifacts that relate to equally destructive conflicts of the past. Armies fighting historic battles wore metallic armor-plating and bold colors to intimidate their opponents. The sight of Orta's hooded mass recalls those battle tactics of the past and exploits the power of uniform to present a provocative message of peace and reconciliation.

Transgressing Fashion #0204 is part of a long-established series of works that Orta describes as *Nexus Architecture*. In this series the artist uses uniform outfits often with umbilical attachments that physically connect individuals together. The *Nexus Architecture intervention* Orta presented at the Johannesburg Biennale in 1997 was created in collaboration with a group of women from a shelter for migrant workers. They took part in a workshop where each woman learned how to cut, sew, and assemble their own suits based on the *Nexus Architecture* template. The women also decorated their suits with images, symbols, patterns, and slogans that related to their own histories and personal experiences.

For the Biennale's opening ceremony the women formed a chain with their brightly colored outfits and marched around the separate exhibition venues. The costumes enabled the women to display individual stories while also making a defiant statement as a unified group. They overturned the traditional function of the uniform, an outfit that removes personal identity, but also exploits its capacity to present an image of unity.

4-152

OPPOSITE AND BELOW EACH WOMAN'S INDIVIDUAL STORY IS REVEALED IN THE DETAIL OF HER OUTFITS, BUT THE IMPRESSION FROM AFAR IS THAT OF A UNIFIED GROUP. DURING THE INTERVENTION IN JOHANNESBURG PASSERS-BY JOINED THE LINE OF WOMEN AND SPONTANEOUSLY BROKE INTO AN IMPROVISED VERSION OF *NKOSI SIKELELE I AFRICA* (*GOD BLESS AFRICA*), A SONG THAT WAS BANNED UNDER APARTHEID.

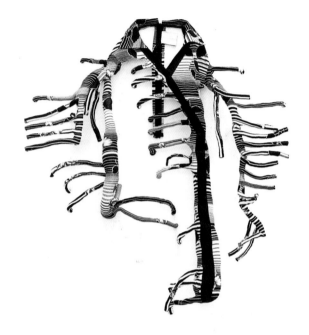

The weight, texture, and weave of a piece of fabric along with the color and pattern imprinted upon it tell us as much about a particular garment, and the person wearing it, as the style in which it is made. Textiles have a language all their own and convey important pieces of information about our age, race, class, and gender.

Munich-based artist Ina Ettlinger is keenly attuned to the dialects and nuances of fabrics. She spends hours on end scrounging through rummage sales, flea markets, and secondhand stores in search of used clothes—typically women's dresses, skirts, tops, or housecoats—that speak to her through their texture and pattern. She is particularly fond of synthetic fibers (perhaps because they are original or because they mimic the identity of natural ones) and bold patterns in waves, stripes, plaids, or organic blobs that scream for attention, or seem to signal an unknown or forgotten message.

Like a scientist or a surgeon, Ettlinger doesn't stop at the collection of rare specimens but takes the analysis a step further by carefully dissecting the clothes she buys. Using her studio as if it were a laboratory, she painstakingly disassembles the garments she considers to be the most interesting and restructures and reconnects them in new ways. By isolating a pattern, cutting it out, sewing it into a form, and stuffing it to become an independent shape, Ettlinger literally deconstructs the clothes and metaphorically

the human body whose form they take. Sometimes an entire garment is broken down into nothing more than the sum of a few new sculptural parts that walk up the walls or spill out onto the floor—as if the article of clothing were simply waiting to be emancipated. Other times only sections of the garment are removed, leaving behind a skeleton or cadaver of sorts, as in an autopsy.

As in an examination of a real human body, the results are both surreal and beautiful. Lines, squares, teardrops, spots, and spirals—from a frumpy housecoat, a groovy mini dress, or an orderly frock—are removed from their unified systems to become autonomous forms with new meanings. Codes are broken down through separation and isolation. The female identity, represented by weave and pattern, is undone, reviewed, and reworked.

As a further step in her process of investigation, Ettlinger is planning to make a series of photographs that document people wearing the clothes post-examination. Simply imagining how these photos might look is an interesting exercise for anyone involved in fashion because it provokes numerous questions about when and where clothing begins and ends. Even so, Ettlinger has never been interested in showing her clothes in a fashion show. For her, they are much more important when they exist in the space of potential, somewhere between picture, sculpture, and material object.

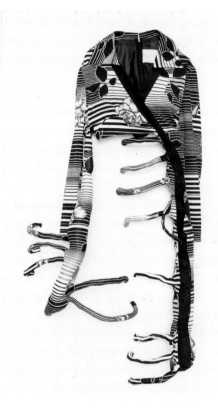

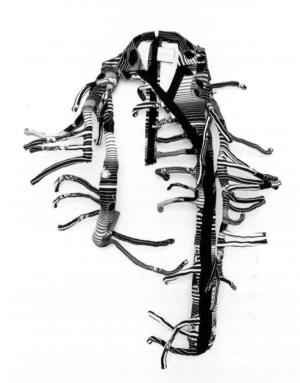

THIS PAGE AND OPPOSITE

MUNICH ARTIST INA ETTLINGER
EXPLORES FEMALE IDENTITY
BY METHODICALLY AND PAINS-
TAKINGLY DECONSTRUCTING
WOMEN'S CLOTHING, IN THIS
CASE A 1970S' DRESS. AS THOUGH
PERFORMING AN AUTOPSY,
ETTLINGER PROBES THE MAKE-UP
AND CONSTRUCTION OF THE
DRESS IN SEVERAL STAGES,
SHOWN HERE IN CHRONOLOGICAL
ORDER AND OPPOSITE AT THE
END OF THE PROCESS.

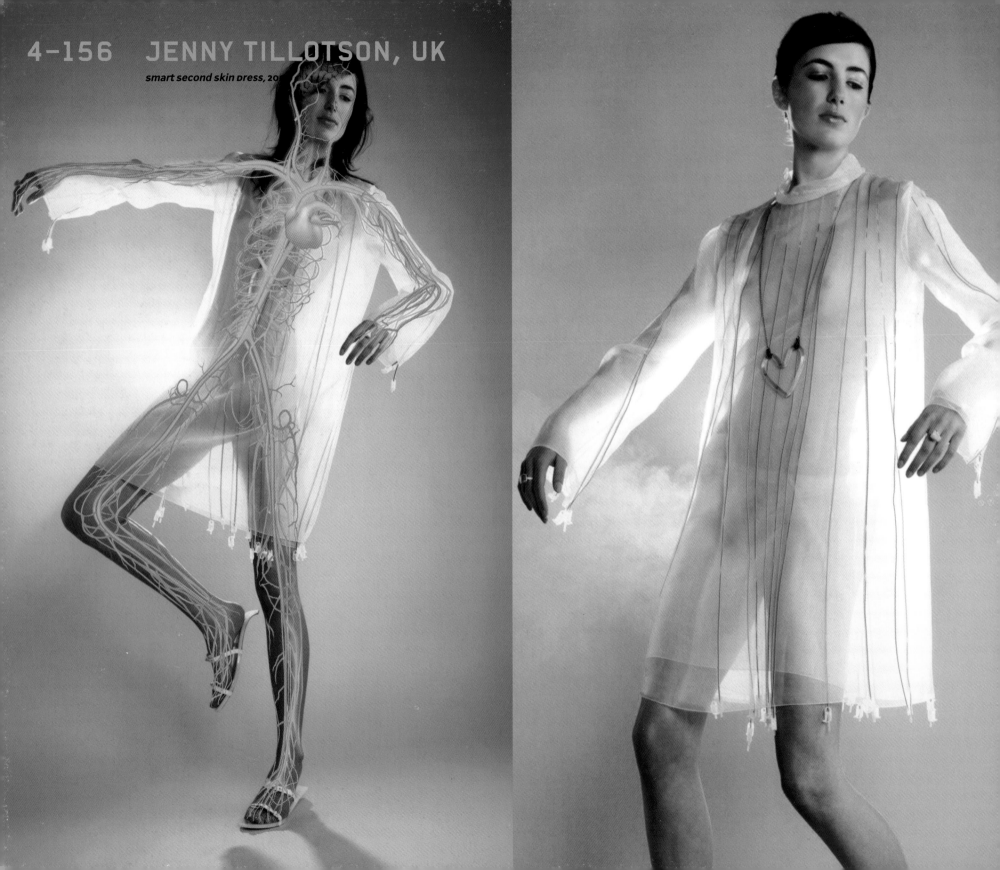

smart second skin dress, 20

Jenny Tillotson, a senior Research Fellow in the Fashion and Design Department of Central St. Martins College in London, is a pioneer of wearable, scent-output systems. According to Tillotson, of all the senses humans possess, our ability to smell receives the least attention in our culture. After seven years of research in aroma technology, Tillotson's *smart second skin dress* is a concrete example of how science, fiction, and fashion can come together in the service of bodily health and psychological well-being.

Also known as *scentorgan dress,* the whispery, mid-thigh tunic is a prototype created by Paris-based fashion designer Adeline André. Like the human body, the garment has its own circulation system, scent glands, and nervous system which allow its wearer to experience and control the different emotional states of the garment. Woven into the dress is a network of medical tubing, resembling the body's own capillaries, which holds colored liquids of differing aromas. A small pump mimics the function of the heart and blood vessels to emit scents which produce and enhance the wearer's olfactory experience. Using this technology, aromatic messages may be pulsed to key points of the body, enabling the user to surround herself with a personally tailored scent bubble.

A spectrum of scents is represented by the colored liquids within the cables. This "rainbow" is a direct reference to the aromas emitted from the "scent organ" in Aldous Huxley's *Brave New world:* "The scent organ was playing a delightfully refreshing Herbal capriccio—rippling arpeggios of thyme and lavender, of rosemary, basil, myrtle, tarragon; a series of daring modulations through the spice keys into ambergis; and a slow return through sandalwood, camphor, cedar, and newmown hay...."

Much of the research in *smart second skin* clothing includes work with pheromones,

aromatic molecules found on our skin which play a role in sexual attraction and serve as chemical messages to those around us. Pheromones are specific to each of us and influence the behavior of those around us. At the moment there are many unanswered questions about whether pheromones are consciously detected or can be programmed. Thus, there are a number of foreseeable social applications for the dress in the future, such as sending scent messages to potential partners.

"The dress paves the way to an expanded life, making the most of what our senses have to offer," says Tillotson. "It increases creativity, expressions and visions, sparks little reminders, expands color, texture, sounds and taste, pushing the boundaries of the senses we didn't know we had.... It transforms negative mood states into good 'scentsations,' releasing scents to help sleep, boost confidence, relax, energize, arouse, increase self-esteem, expand the imagination, and open your sense of wonder."

LEFT AND OPPOSITE THE *SMART SECOND SKIN* DRESS IS A REVOLUTIONARY PROTOTYPE GARMENT THAT DELIVERS AROMAS TO DIFFERENT PARTS OF THE BODY. LIKE OUR OWN SKIN, THE DRESS IS CABLED WITH "VEINS"—IN THIS INSTANCE, MEDICAL TUBING FASTENED AT THE ENDS BY SURGICAL CLAMPS—WHICH HOLD AND RELEASE COLORED SCENTS.

BIBLIOGRAPHY

INTRODUCTION

Amies, Hardy. *The Englishman's suit*. London: Quartet Books, 1994.

cannon, Peter. "welcome to LA: sudden Death in olympic city." *The Face*, issue 50, London: June 1984.

Fricke, Jim, Charlie Ahearn, Nelson George. *yes yes y'all: the Experience Music Project oral History of Hip Hop's First Decade*. New York: Da capo Press, 2002.

Garcia, Bobbito. *where'd you Get Those?: New York city's sneaker culture: 1960–1987*. New York: Powerhouse Books, 2003.

Godfrey, John (ed.). *A Decade of I-Deas 1980–1990*. Harmondsworth, UK: Penguin Books, 1990.

Polhemus, Ted (victoria and Albert Museum). *street style: From sidewalk to catwalk*. London: Thames and Hudson, 1994.

Toop, David. "The Beatbox Bites Back." *The Face*, issue 49, London: June 1984.

wilcox, Claire. *vivienne westwood*. London: V&A Publications, 2004.

CHAPTER 1
STREET LIFE

marlan, Toni. "Elements of style: Getting a charge out of a Bag." *chicago Reader*, July 25, 2003, section 1, p. 31.

navratil, wendy. "Thinking outside the Grid: solar-charged cell Phones." *chicago Tribune*, July 27, 2003.

Bolton, Andrew. *supermodern wardrobe*. London: V&A Publications, 2002.

quinn, Bradley. *The Fashion of Architecture*. oxford, UK: Berg, 2003.

kamphuis, Hanneke. "needlework." *Frame*, issue 36, Amsterdam, Netherlands: January/February 2004.

mohlo, Renata. "transformables." *Abitare*, issue 405, Milan: April 2001.

welch, Jilly. "Living in the Hood." *Blueprint*, issue 211, chelmsford, UK: september 2003.

CHAPTER 2
BEHIND A PAINTED SMILE

Abbas, Remi. "masked by Nature." *Blueprint*, issue 219, chelmsford, UK: May 2004.

Burkeman, oliver. "The Bush Baiters." *The Guardian*, London, November 2, 2004.

Post, Peggy. *Emily Post's wedding Etiquette*. New York: Harpercollins, 2001, pp. 239–40.

thompson, Nato. *The Interventionists: users' manual for the creative Disruption of Everyday Life*. Boston: MIT Press, 2004.

wenzel, Erik. "That was Now, This Then" *F News magazine*, The school of the Art Institute of chicago, December 2002.

CHAPTER 3
TO PROTECT AND TO SERVE

"**corpo Nove**," Press release. www.corponove.it

Lupton, Ellen. *skin*. New York: Princeton Architectural Press, 2002, pp. 180, 182.

Nakamura, Akemi. "Robot suit a culmination of sci-fi Dreams." *The Japan Times online*, Tokyo: August 13, 2004.

CHAPTER 4
DRESS CODE

Lenander, Johanna. "sticky." *zoo Magazin*, p. 30.

Nolan, Billy. "stretching the Imagination." *Frame*, London, issue 39, 2004, pp. 16–17.

Pinto, Roberto, Nicolas Bourriaud, Maia Damianovic. *Lucy orta*. London: Phaidon, 2003.

"**Rubén ortiz Torres—The Texas Leaguer**." Exhibition press release, Glassell school of Art, January 15–March 7, 2004.

schouwenberg, Louise. "A Life Less ordinary." *Frame*, issue 24, Amsterdam, Netherlands: January/February 2002.

EXHIBITIONS

Boys Who Sew. curated by Prof. Janis Jefferies. Crafts Council Gallery, London, october 18–January 6, 2004.

Kyochi Tsuzuki: Happy Victims. curated by Michael Mallard. The Photographers Gallery, London, september 25–November 16, 2003.

Radical Fashion. curated by Claire Wilcox. Victoria & Albert Museum, London, october 18, 2001–January 6, 2002.

The Fashion of Architecture. curated by Bradley Quinn. The Deluxe Gallery, London, February 12–21, 2004.

Breakin Convention: An International Festival of Hip Hop Dance Theatre. curated by Jonzi D. Sadler's Wells Theatre, London, May 15–16, 2004.

WEB & E-MAIL ADDRESSES

Jurgen Bey: www.jurgenbey.nl
Center for Tactical Magic:
   www.tacticalmagic.org
Corpo Nove: www.corponove.it
Dungeon Majesty: www.dungeonmajesty.com
Engarde: www.engardebodyarmor.com
Ina Ettlinger: inaettlinger@web.de
Alexandra Fede: www.alexandrafede.com
Moreno Ferrari: mo.ferrari@libero.it
Alicia Framis: www.annetgelink.com
Christopher J. Glaister & Michelle Shakallis:
   www.barcodetextiles.com
Cookie Gluck: www.cookiegluck.com
Paddy Hartley: www.paddyhartley.com
Hoodlum Welding Gear:
   www.hoodlum-welding.com
House of Harlot: www.house-of-harlot.com
JAM: www.jamwork.com
Kei Kagami: kei@kagami.freeserve.co.uk
Greg Leong: gleong@tassie.net.au
Josh MacPhee: www.justseeds.org
Anne Niemetz: www.adime.de
Lucy Orta: www.studio-orta.com
Yuka Oyama: www.dearyuka.com
Martina Salzberger:
   martina_salzberger@web.de
Yoshiyuki Sankai: www.cyberdyne.jp
Grit & Jerszy Seymour: www.gritseymour.com
Stuart Sproule: www.stuartsproule.com
Wolfgang Stehle: wolfi.stehle@gmx.de
Susumu Tachi: www.star.t.u-tokyo.ac.jp
Temporary Services:
   www.temporaryservices.org
Jenny Tillotson:
   www.smartsecondskin.com/main/
   scentorgandress
Tommy the Clown: http://tommytheclown.com
Manel Torres: www.fabricanltd.com
Rubén Ortiz Torres: rubenot@sbcglobal.net
Vexed Generation: www.vexed.co.uk
Visual Kei Fans: www.jjstratford.com
Adam Whiton & Yolita Nugent:
   www.no-contact.com
Stefan Wishnewski: wischnewski@gmx.net
Krzysztof Wodiczko: wodiczko@mit.edu
The Yes Men: www.theyesmen.org
Yomango: www.yomango.net

PHOTO CREDITS

All reasonable efforts have been made to obtain copyright permission for the images in this book. If we have committed an oversight, we will be pleased to rectify it in a subsequent edition.

Front cover: *TAPE* spring/summer 2004 collection by Grit + Jerszy Seymour. Photos by Karen Ann Donnachie. Art direction by Andy Simionato; hair & make-up by Gabriele Trezzi/Close Up Milano; model: Taylor/ICE Models Milano

Frontispiece: Alicia Framis, *Anti_Dog Parnassia*, 2003

p. 9 top left: photo by Jacques Henri Lartigue/© Ministère de la Culture, France/AAJHL; top right: Niall McInerney

p. 11 top left: © OMA; bottom left: Paramount/Kobal Collection; right: © Paco Rabanne

p. 13 top left and right: courtesy Galerie Bernhard Knaus, Mannheim/© VG Bild-Kunst, Bonn 2004; bottom left: © Leif Skoogfors/Corbis; bottom center: © Vauthey Pierre/Corbis Sygma

p. 15 top left: photo by Karin Seufert; top center: photo by Valentina Seidl; bottom right: photo by Lauren Greenfield/VII

p. 17 top left: photo by Jennifer Juniper Stratford; bottom left: photo by Martha Cooper; right: © Bettmann/Corbis

pp. 18–19 © Veronika Kapsali

pp. 24–27 photos by Belinda Lawley

pp. 28–31 photos by Juan Mendez and Stuart Sproule; illustration by Stuart Sproule

pp. 40–43 photos by Becky Coppelia Lee except p. 40 bottom center by Yuri Yoshida

pp. 44–45 photos by /courtesy of Temporary Services & Rob Kelly and Zena Sakowski

pp. 46–47 work: Temporary Services & Rob Kelly and Zena Sakowski

pp. 48–49 courtesy of JAM

pp. 50–53 Vexed Generation

pp. 54–55 photos by Rebecca Harman

pp. 60–61 photos by Jennifer Juniper Stratford

p. 62 right: Cameron Gainer

p. 63 Cameron Gainer

pp. 64–65 video and photos by Wolfgang Stehle

pp. 66–67 Tachi Laboratory, University of Tokyo

pp. 68–71 Paddy Hartley in collaboration with Dr. Ian Thompson, biomaterials scientist, King's College, London

p. 72 © design, modeling, and photography by Mercedes & Gen, 2004

p. 73 rubber costumes created by House of Harlot. Photos © Perou at www.perouinc.com

pp. 74–75 © design, modeling, and photography by Mercedes & Gen, 2004

pp. 76–77 Josh MacPhee

pp. 78–79 Daniel Schwerdtfeger

p. 80 © McDermott & McGough

p. 81 © McDermott & McGough. Top left and right: courtesy Galerie Jérôme de Noirmont, Paris

pp. 82–83 The Yes Men

pp. 86–89 Dungeon Majesty

pp. 94–95 http://www.hoodlum-welding.com

pp. 96–97 Alexandra Fede

pp. 98–99 founder of Cyberdyne Inc.: Professor Sankai http://www.cyberdyne.jp Cybernics, Robot Suit HAL (Hybrid Assistive Limb), University of Tsukuba, Cyberdyne

pp. 100–103 Stefan Wischnewski

p. 104–5 photos by Eric Michelot

p. 106–7 photo by Marianne Rosenthiel

pp. 108–109 Marco Gozzani

pp. 110–111 © Engarde Body Armor

pp. 112–13 photos by Oliver Jung

p. 115 photos by Oliver Jung

pp. 118–119 Yolita Nugent and Adam Whiton

p. 124 photos by Pam Zeplin

pp. 125–127 photos by Gregory Leong

pp. 128–131 photos by Bill Short

pp. 134–136 photos by Karen Ann Donnachie. Art direction: Andy Simionato; hair & make-up: Gabriele Trezzi/Close Up Milano; models: Taylor/ICE Models Milano, Patrick/Fashion Milano

p. 137 photo by Marc Domage

pp. 138–141 photos by Tommo London, at@tommophoto.com. Hair stylist: Ernesto Montenovo; make-up: Claudine Anderson; stylist: Ryo Araki; model: Olga Lebedeva @ ISIS Models, London

pp. 144–47 courtesy of Cookie Gluck www.cookiegluck.com

pp. 148–49 photos by Richard Greenhill

p. 151 photos by Jason Evans

pp. 154–55 Ina Ettlinger

pp. 156–57 concept by Jenny Tillotson PhD RCA FION, senior research fellow, Central Saint Martins College of Art & Design. Dress by Adeline Andre; photos by Guy Hills

p. 156 left: as above and image by Wendy Latham; right: as above and hair & make-up by Louise Heywood @ Artistic Licence

p. 157 left: as above and hair & make-up by Anne-Marie Simak @ Artistic Licence; right: image by Jenny Tillotson

and copyright © the individual artists

THE AUTHORS AND PUBLISHER ARE VERY GRATEFUL TO THE FOLLOWING FOR THEIR HELP IN THE CREATION OF THIS BOOK:

FOR HELP AND ADVICE
HARRY ALLEN; ZANE BERZINA; AVA BROMBERG; JORDI CLARAMONTE, LAS AGENCIAS; KIM COPE;
HELEN COSTELLO; ANDREW HANSEN; NICOLA HARENBERG; JO HODDER AND THE SOCIETY OF AUTHORS; PHILIPPA HURD;
ROB LUTTON; MARGARET MCHUGH; KAROLIN MAIER-HAUFF; GERBRAND VON NIJENDAAL; EMMANUELLE DE NOIRMONT;
FRANK POLLEY, HENRI PLUS FRANK PR; SABINE SCHMID; STUART SMITH, SMITH DESIGN; NATO THOMPSON;
HENRY THOMPSON, MIKE AND CHARLOTTE WILSON, AND ALL THE REPS; TOMMO.

CONTRIBUTORS
ALFREDO, ALEXANDRA FEDE; ROBIN ARCHER, HOUSE OF HARLOT; PAUL BANNISTER, YOMANGO; VICTORIA BERRY;
MARGRIET, JURGEN BEY; BRETT BLOOM AND TEMPORARY SERVICES; MIKE BONNANO, THE YES MEN; CORPO NOVE;
CHRISTINE, JENNIFER, LIZA, SARAH, AND RILEY, DUNGEON MAJESTY; ENGARDE; INA ETTLINGER;
MARIANNE FAIRBANKS AND JANE PALMER, JAM; ALICIA FRAMIS; AARON GACH, CENTER FOR TACTICAL MAGIC;
CHRISTOPHER J.GLAISTER AND MICHELLE SHAKALLIS; COOKIE GLUCK; REBECCA HARMAN; PADDY HARTLEY AND IAN THOMPSON;
HOODLUM WELDING GEAR; KEI KAGAMI; VERONIKA KAPSALI; BELINDA LAWLEY; GREG LEONG; JOSH MACPHEE;
DAVID MCDERMOTT & PETER MCGOUGH; MERCEDES AND GEN; ANNE NIEMETZ; YUKA OYAMA; MARTINA SALZBERGER;
YOSHIYUKI SANKAI; MARIKO SAWATA, SUSUMU TACHI; GRIT & JERSZY SEYMOUR; STUART SPROULE;
JENNIFER JUNIPER STRATFORD; WOLFGANG STEHLE; JENNY TILLOTSON, SMART SECOND SKIN; TOMMY THE CLOWN;
MANEL TORRES, FABRICAN; RUBÉN ORTIZ TORRES; VEXED GENERATION; STEFAN WISCHNEWSKI; KRZYSZTOF WODICZKO.

COURTENAY SMITH
A SPECIAL THANK YOU TO STEFAN EBERSTADT FOR HIS CONSTANT SUPPORT AND GUIDANCE.

SEAN TOPHAM
AND FINALLY AN EXTRA SPECIAL THANK YOU TO SALLY RICKABY AND TO ALL MY FRIENDS AND FAMILY
FOR THEIR CONTINUING SUPPORT AND GOOD WISHES.